This Ragged Place

Other books by Terry Glavin

A DEATH FEAST IN DIMLAHAMID (1990)

NEMIAH: THE UNCONQUERED COUNTRY
(*with Gary Fiegehen, Rick Blacklaws, Vance Hanna,
and the People of Nemiah Valley*) (1992)

A GHOST IN THE WATER (1994)

DEAD RECKONING: CONFRONTING THE CRISIS
IN PACIFIC FISHERIES (1996)

TERRY GLAVIN

THIS RAGGED PLACE

Travels Across the Landscape

NEW STAR BOOKS

VANCOUVER

1996

Picture credits: Page 2, Alan Sirulnikoff; p. 22 , Alex Waterhouse-Hayward; pp. 40, 188, Ulli Steltzer; p. 66, Rick Waines; p. 80, Xero; p. 108, Arlen Redekop/ *Province*; p. 122, Steve Bosch; p. 170, Gary Fiegehen.

Martin Dunphy: editing
Rolf Maurer, Audrey McClellan: production
Printed and bound in Canada by Webcom Ltd.
1 2 3 4 5   00 99 98 97 96

Publication of this book is made possible by grants from the Canada Council and the Cultural Services Branch, Province of British Columbia.

CANADIAN CATALOGUING IN PUBLICATION DATA
Glavin, Terry, 1955-
  This ragged place

  ISBN 0-921586-52-3

  1. British Columbia – Social conditions. 2. British Columbia – History – 1945-
I. Title.
FC3818.G42 1996   971.1'04   C96-910676-9

Contents

Acknowledgments

It was a long road.

Along the way, there were many people, young and old, Native and Settler, whose stories shaped this book just as certainly as their their own lives were shaped by the mountains and the rivers traversed within these pages. This is their book, just as surely as this is their country.

This book does not attempt to answer any big questions about British Columbia's history, or about British Columbia's unique and arguably distinct society, or where this province fits within Canada. This book does not propose to approach that question that is routinely alleged to so preoccupy Canadians: Who are we?

That may be an important question elsewhere, for important people to raise. On this side of the Rockies, there is another question that remains: Where are we, anyway?

The title of this book is taken from a poem by Howie White. Charles Campbell, editor of the *Georgia Straight*, graciously allowed much of this book to be published in essay form while the work was progressing over the past four years. I am deeply grateful for the tremendous help provided by Martin Dunphy, my editor; New Star's publisher, Rolf Maurer, who is also a dear friend; as well as New Star's Carolyn Stewart and Audrey McClellan, for their guidance and advice.

I am particularly grateful to Chief Diane Bailey, and to Rick Bailey, and to all the other Baileys, Adamses, Pierres, Florences, Jameses, Millers, and all the others at Katzie, for their friendship and kindness; and to Barry and Nancy Manuck, for the same.

But most of all, this book is for my wife, Yvette Guigueno, and our children, Zoe, Eamonn and Conall. I love you more than you will ever know.

This Ragged Place

The Skeena Run

I am well aware that this plan may scare the timid and frighten the irresolute. But I may claim that every man who has in his bosom a stout Canadian heart will welcome it as worthy of this young nation.

— PRIME MINISTER WILFRID LAURIER, 1903

In the minutes before the train pulled away from the old station, a gang of elk, part of a herd that winters around Jasper for fear of wolves, ambled through the rail yard and jaywalked across the broad boulevard of Connaught Drive. After a moment of indecision, four of the animals turned back and returned to the rail yard, where they trudged slowly and in single file eastward along the rail line in view of the sushi bar at Tokyo Tom's Place and the tables at Papa George's. Two stayed and grazed in the grass by the Jasper National Park visitors centre. A few steps away, Japanese tourists snapped their cameras at them. The young Australian tourists continued playing hackysack, apparently no longer impressed by such close-up scenes of Canadian wildlife.

The train was empty but for the crew and a mere handful of travellers who boarded at the station, which seemed odd, this being the departure point for a renowned 1,000-kilometre rail excursion, with its terminus at Prince Rupert, that is ranked among the most breathtaking and intriguing rail journeys in the world. Night was falling, and the mountains were draped in rain and cloud when the train lurched forward to begin its long, rumbling ascent into the Selwyn Range of the Rocky Mountains, toward Yellowhead Pass. Yellowhead Pass, from Yellow Head, or Tête Jaune, or Tay John.

It is at the summit of the pass that British Columbia begins, at precisely that place where the little creeks and streams that feed into the Miette and the Athabasca and, ultimately, the Arctic Ocean give way, at Mile 17.5, to the creeks and streams that tumble down through their craggy watersheds to feed the Fraser River and, ultimately, the Pacific Ocean. But there has always been another kind of border up there somewhere, between what is real and what is imagined. Nobody is certain how the place even got its name.

There is a remote possibility that Yellow Head (Tête Jaune, Tay John) was the fur trader François Decoigne, who was known for his bright blond hair, but about whom little record remains beyond a dot on the map, Decoigne, a few minutes into the journey west of Jasper. But it is almost certain that the real Tay John was Pierre Hatsinaton, a blond-haired Iroquois trapper and hunting guide, one of several Iroquois "freemen" who explored and settled in the northern Rockies. Hatsinaton ventured through the gap in the mountains and was killed, along with his family, by a party of Beaver Indians on the Rockies' western slopes, near Tête Jaune Cache on the upper reaches of the Fraser River, in 1827.

Yellowhead Pass is perhaps less majestic than the Kicking Horse or the Crowsnest, the Rocky Mountains' southerly portals. The route was regarded by the North West Company and the Hudson's Bay Company as a passage of particular hardship. Among other things, it meant crossing paths with Snake Indians and Assiniboines. Still, it was through the Yellowhead Pass that Jasper Hawes ascended, after a quarter century as a trader with the North West Company (it was his name the railroad camp formerly known as Fitzhugh took for itself). Jasper Hawes was drawn westward in 1825. That year, he and his family packed their belongings into a canoe and portaged across Yellowhead Pass for the Fraser's headwaters. They were never seen again.

It was through this pass that the Overlanders of 1862 also came, looking for their own El Dorado in the form of placer gold in the Cariboo mines. They came all the way from what was then Canada, and by the time they trudged through Yellowhead Pass and confronted the gulf between what was real and what they had imagined, they were half mad, living off skunk meat and begging from whatever Indians they encountered. Four of them died making the last leg to Quesnel. Half of them gave up before they got to the Cariboo, heading south to New Westminster and Victoria. Several left for home straightaway, by ship, around Cape Horn. As the story goes, only one of the party of 131 ever found any gold.

There is yet another Yellow Head who bears mention, whose universe begins to unravel about the time the first railroad crews were blasting their way through these mountains in the early years of this century. He is the central character in Howard

O'Hagan's 1939 novel, *Tay John*, one of British Columbia's strangest and most disturbing works of literature. The novel plays itself out here, among these mountains and within the pass through the Rockies that the train ascended, slowly rumbling westward. O'Hagan's Tay John is an infant-shaman who emerges from the newly dug grave of the young Shuswap woman who died pregnant with him. Tay John lives his life burdened by his people's hopes that he will fulfil a tribal prophecy and lead them westward, out of these mountains to a long-lost promised land, somewhere to the west. Michael Ondaatje would have us see O'Hagan's Tay John this way: "He is given new names in every setting and he slides through all his roles like water. He leaves only fragments of his myth behind; he has no cause or motive or moral to announce, and as a result is of no worth in the new societies of commerce, religion, and imperialism."

When the train rumbled into Yellowhead Pass with a passenger list only six names long, a number not even equal to the seven on the crew list, it was impossible to avoid worrying just a little about the legacy begun in 1902 with Charles Melville Hays and his Grand Trunk Railway, continued after 1920 by Canadian National Railways, and assumed by Via Rail in 1978 when the CNR and Canadian Pacific Railway amalgamated their passenger services under the aegis of a Crown corporation. It was too easy to imagine that the Yellowhead Route – or the Skeena Run, as Via Rail calls it, or the Rupert Rocket, as it is known to people along the line – is of absolutely no worth in the new societies of commerce, religion, and imperialism (or of highways, airplanes, and television, for that matter). On the other hand, it might have been because of the doldrums between the ski season and the summer. And there would be several more passengers to pick up along the way, after all.

At any rate, nothing dramatic happened when the train reached the summit. The blue mountains disappeared into the dark and the sky turned slowly from grey to black. At this time of year and at this time of day, it is impossible to see Mount Robson (the highest point in the Rocky Mountains), and the towering cedar and hemlock forests, out there in the night somewhere, are left to the imagination. So, by the time the train had begun its westward descent from Yellowhead Pass, the few passengers settled down in the restored 1955 art-deco Skyline car for a drink, or they turned in for the night, and the only view of the landscape left was through the narrow windshields at the head of the engine, in a compartment designed in the same proportions as the wheelhouse of a gillnet boat, where engineer John Howarth, in engineer's overalls, and assistant conductor John Small, in sharp assistant-conductor's uniform, maintained their long watch, staring out into the tunnel of light the train's headlamp punched through the darkened countryside.

We passed Fitzwilliam and Grant Brook and Moose Lake, then the train switched off the main transcontinental tracks at Redpass, to head northwest through tangled forests of aspen and alder and kinnikinnick, toward Prince Rupert.

It's the quiet season, Small said. And this was a particularly quiet night. At this time of year, there were usually eight or ten passengers in the sleeping car and ten or twelve in the coach, but even those numbers were far lower than they could be, Small reckoned. He called Via's Skeena Run "absolutely the finest route in the country", and it was hard to imagine that he would be wrong. The summer before, the route was packed with Thomas Cook tours from England, and without benefit of much concerted marketing, it seemed to rely almost solely on local traffic and a word-of-mouth reputation around the world. "This

train has the potential to be twenty cars long all year round,"
Small said, leaning back in his cockpit seat. "If it were marketed
the right way." A great circle route – by rail from Vancouver to
Jasper and Jasper to Prince Rupert, ferry to Port Hardy, bus to
Courtenay, Via's "Malahat" to Victoria, and ferry to Vancouver
again – could showcase the Skeena Run, but it was a difficult trip
for the travel agents to package. The connections could get complicated. Whether or not it was a case of lost marketing opportunities, on this night the 2,000-horsepower General Motors
F40PH-2 diesel locomotive was pulling only a dining car, a sleeping car/coach, and the Skyline car. Things are changing, Small
said. Howarth said yes, things are changing.

Both of their fathers were train engineers, and their fathers
saw steam give way to diesel, but that was nothing like the
changes these two had seen. Howarth and Small saw the aban-
donment of the old Uniform Code of Operating Rules, an elaborate body of law and custom that governed the culture of the
railway throughout North America. The rules had remained
largely unchanged for a century by the time Howarth and Small
took up this life in the late 1960s. Every twenty miles or so there
was a station with an operator and his orders. Communication
between the stations was still by the old telegraph keys, operated
by the members of the Order of Railroad Telegraphers. Nobody
trusted radios. As recently as 1989, the station operators used
the "train order hoop" on the Skeena line. It was little more than
a bamboo stick with its end shaped in the form of a "v," and
attached to it by a length of string were amended schedules for
passing trains. The engineer would pass a station, reach his arm
out the window, and hook the device as the train roared by the
whistle-stop. "You got pretty good at it," Howarth said. "Eventually." Eastbound trains were always even-numbered, and west-

bound trains were odd-numbered. Eastbound always had priority, unless it was a passenger train. You were constantly checking your time, "and there were some real eyelash meets," Howarth recalled. "Roaring to a station you knew you only had minutes to make, and then an air hose blows," which meant the brakeman had to run ahead, sometimes for several miles, to lay small explosive charges on the tracks to alert the engineer in the oncoming train that he should expect to see a flagman up ahead.

Eventually, radios became more reliable and better-trusted. Soon the caboose was gone. The old customs began to break down, and then there were fewer jobs. Even the sound of the railway was changing – the clickity click, clickity click sound a train made as it passed over each piece of track, each thirty-eight feet in length, was giving way as new sections of rail, a quarter-mile long, were spooled out along the lines to replace rusty rails. All of which meant fewer jobs still.

Howarth, a member of the Brotherhood of Locomotive Engineers, had worked on this line with Via for six years. Before that, he ran CN's freight trains on this same line for twelve years. He started out at the Kamloops yards in 1969, the year eight railway workers died in a derailment. Derailments were common. Howarth remembered old Emmot Desorcey, an engineer who had "been in the river" no fewer than nine times in his career. The way these things happened was straightforward enough. There would be a rockslide on the rails, the train engine would crash into it and tumble down a steep embankment into the Thompson or the Fraser, and you'd live or you'd die. But by the 1990s, there were slide detectors along the line that lit up a series of lamps along the tracks if there were rocks up ahead. Just as Howarth was reminiscing about the old bamboo train-order hoops, a weird little computerized voice broke into the conversation from a speaker above his head: "CN detector mileage twelve Fraser sub no alarms." It was transmitted from a high-tech "hotbox", one of a series of devices located at intervals along the rail line that assessed the state of each of the train's steel wheels as they rumbled along the tracks, and reported by cybervoice to the engineer in the train. If a wheel's bearings were shot, the weird little voice came into the engine compartment to tell the engineer which wheel had a problem.

Howarth kept his eyes peeled anyway. "I remember winters when there were 150 moose kills on 120 miles of track on this line," he said. "And one winter there were forty caribou killed during a single snowplow run."

And you never knew. There could have been somebody on the line waiting for a lift. But that was changing too. When Howarth and Small took up a life on the rails, there were about two hundred flag stations along the Skeena line, although it's true there was only the occasional cause to pick up or put down a passenger at many of them. For a time, during the 1960s, there was a brief resurgence in flag-stop traffic as hippies started moving back to the land and Americans began settling into the remote corners of B.C.'s north woods, hiding away from the war in Vietnam. "But that's pretty well dead now," Howarth said. Where the hippies hadn't moved away, the logging roads had pushed through, and by 1995 only a handful of the thirty-odd remaining flag stations between Jasper and Prince Rupert were truly railonly, totally inaccessible by road. At Longworth, a faction favoured a road and a faction opposed the idea. "But there's a road now," Howarth said. "It's really lost its magic."

As the train pulled into McBride at 11:10 p.m., the Great Law of the Railroad was broken before our very eyes. The now-dead law stipulated that you never left a red switch turned against a main-line passenger train, but a red switch, like a little stop sign that indicates the track is switched to direct the train off the main line, was turned against us as the train pulled up to McBride station. Howarth and Small peered out into the night, looking for Tom O'Connor, who had flagged them down on the eastbound leg at Penny two mornings ago to make the two-hour trip east to McBride for his monthly shopping excursion. Now O'Connor was heading home.

"Where's old Tom?" Small asked.

"I don't know," Howarth answered, "but I can see his groceries."

Eventually, Tom pulled himself away from whoever he was chatting with in the station and climbed into the Skyline car, and Small climbed down and opened the switch to keep the train on its westbound tracks. "It just seems so odd, still," Small said as the train pulled out of the station, "to see a red switch open, and nobody there standing beside it."

What the Skeena Run meant to Tom O'Connor was

about the same thing this country's railroads meant to people in small-town Canada from the late 1800s well into this century. The railroad was the only link with the outside world. That's what it still meant to O'Connor that night, and it was the only link O'Connor wanted. In the two hours it took to carry him and his groceries back home to Penny, all he let on about Penny was that its population was nine when he left earlier in the week; that about five years earlier he'd bought a small piece of land with a workshop and a couple of outbuildings and a drafty old house that had been built during the Depression, all for about $12,000; that there was a school at Penny that closed down a couple of years earlier when the population was much larger (about twenty people), and that there had been a sawmill in the vicinity some decades before that. "I don't need electricity," O'Connor snapped. "I don't need television. I got out of those habits a long time ago. I've had my nose busted seven times. I got tired of being great. I couldn't handle it anymore."

What this train meant to him was that he could get in and out of McBride, preferably out, as easily as he needed to. It also meant Via Rail bent its rules for him a bit, like letting him carry on a bicycle, since, after all, the train is the only way in and out of Penny. The story about the bicycle went this way.

O'Connor's custom was to travel to the Okanagan in the summer to pick fruit, and at the end of one season, a fellow fruit picker in a neighbouring shack gave him a bicycle. "I hadn't ridden a bicycle since I was ten years old. So I just hopped on the bike and rode it for about ten miles, wobbly all the way. Then I rode it for about six or seven hours. I got used to it. It took me five days from Kelowna to McBride, and I put on about six pounds in five days. I felt great. I felt like a million dollars. Every night I picked a tree beside a stream. I bought some booze and I'd get shitfaced. My father used to tell me, 'There's no point in spending $30 on a hotel room every night when you can spend $5 on a bottle and sleep anywhere.' He was right."

The only reason he gave for moving to Penny was that he had lived everywhere else. "Like there," he said, pointing to the map of British Columbia in the Skyline car. He got up and walked up to the map and stabbed his finger on a jagged inlet about one-third of the way up British Columbia's coast. "That's Phillips Arm right there." The story about Phillips Arm, where he ran a trapline and kept a cabin next to a logging camp, involved a fourteen-and-a-half-foot boat with a seven-and-a-half-horsepower Mercury outboard and nineteen gallons of gas. It was just before Christmas. "The boys wanted me to make a booze run. So I went down and I got twelve forty-pounders. Whiskey, vodka, all the good stuff."

On his way home, he stopped in at a fish farm where a buddy of his worked as a diver. It was raining in sheets. They got into the bottles, but at about 3 a.m. he decided it was time to get back home. He staggered down the float and stepped onto the transom and a ton of rainwater that had accumulated in the boat rushed astern and over he went. He was carrying a flashlight, which his friend, the diver, watched on its way down into the depths. O'Connor reckoned he hit bottom at about thirty feet. "So I shine the flashlight around and I say to myself, 'Hey, I'm surrounded by fucking water.' So I let out some bubbles to see which way was up, and I followed the bubbles." The diver got his gear on and went down and fished the remaining bottles out of the drink, "so when we make it back to the camp, he's the hero. I'm nobody."

That's the way life is. And it means this: "By the time we think we have everything cased, you know, that's when you find out you don't. The important thing about living is not feeling important; it's feeling needed. I've felt that, many times. I'm blessed. I think I'm pretty right in thinking that I am blessed in being ignorant. So at home, if things get a little short, I'll eat a few more dandelion leaves or something. It doesn't hurt me any. You can take the root and cut it into strips and brown it in the oven, or you can take the leaves, which are high in vitamins, and eat them raw, and you can make wine from the flowers."

O'Connor's stories unfolded, each in turn, as the train passed Goat River, Loos, Urling, and Dome Creek, following the Fraser River as it gathers momentum and gathers tributaries like Twin

Creek and Snowshoe Creek and all the other creeks that pour down from the northern flanks of the Cariboo Mountains, around which the Fraser bends in a wide, sweeping arc, until it was 1:15 a.m. and the train slowed to a stop at Penny. O'Connor gathered his things and said his goodbyes. He shone his flashlight out the open door of the Skyline car and grumbled as he tried to get a fix on the trail through the woods to his house. He couldn't find it. The train shunted back and forth until O'Connor's flashlight picked up a tree that he recognized and he shouted out, and the signal was radioed up to the head of the engine. Howarth pulled up on the throttle and O'Connor climbed down, reaching back for his bags of groceries, and one by one they were handed down to him until there were no more. The train pulled away. O'Connor disappeared into the pitch-black night.

By dawn, the train was well past Prince George, and it was clear by the rolling plateau country out the window that the train was past Vanderhoof and Fort Fraser, too, probably around Endako somewhere. Via's roomettes were as comfortable as sleeping compartments were likely to get, and the rhythm of the train rocks you back to sleep after waking you up now and then. After some initial morning disorientation, it was over a leisurely and pleasant breakfast in the dining car that I found myself remembering another morning in this same countryside, when I stumbled out of a bleak roadside motel into a rental car to look for a café somewhere on the road to Hazelton. The memory of that morning made it much easier to appreciate travelling this way.

All of this was a far cry from the mornings enjoyed by the people who built this stretch of track, of course. The man generally credited with building the entire Grand Trunk edifice is Charles Melville Hays of Rock Island, Illinois, founder of the Grand Trunk Pacific. Like the yellow-haired Pierre Hatsinaton, Jasper Hawes, and the Overlanders of 1862, Hays never lived to see what would become of his vision. He went down with the *Titanic* in 1912. He should be credited with bringing in air brakes to replace the hand brakes that maimed so many railway workers, and we know his name, at least, which is more than most railroad histories have done for the thirty men who died in a single rock blast at Boer Mountain, just west of Endako. The year Hays drowned in the North Atlantic, 3,000 workers on this very section of track, between Endako and Hazelton, walked off the job under the banner of the anarchist Industrial Workers of the World, demanding wages of $3 for an eight-hour day. The *Vancouver Sun* reported: "Two hundred miles of the railroad it is said are under control of these restless spirits and serious trouble is looked for." The *Sun* carried reports of armed IWW organizers, widespread conspiracies, threats, and menaces to peace and order. The *Sun* did not mention that its publisher, J. W. Stewart, was a partner in Foley, Welch and Stewart, one of the more notorious railroad contractors of the day, a source of much of the initial discontent on the Grand Trunk and the prime strikebreaker credited with bringing the dispute to an end.

But I wasn't going to let all that ruin my breakfast. Besides, the sun was breaking through the clouds, only patches of snow covered the spruce hills, and the ice was melting in the moose swamps. The train was passing Burns Lake, Decker Lake, and Palling, rumbling through, or at least toward, a boundary of sorts, albeit an event a lot less stirring than Yellowhead Pass. The summit here is indiscernible, only a meandering height of land that marks the place where the creeks no longer flow to the east into the Endako, the Nechako, and the Fraser rivers, but instead flow to the west, down into the Bulkley and the Skeena rivers. When it happens here, in this country, it does not involve cascading waterfalls and great ruptures in the very crust of the earth. It occurs quietly, beneath the lilies that are strewn all over the surface of Rose Lake, about halfway between Decker Lake and, say, Topley. Half of Rose Lake empties east, the other half empties west, and that's all there is to it. There is only a gradual emergence of something that has changed, and it first appears in the west, then to the south and the north. It is a noticeable raggedness about the horizon that becomes obvious about the time the train passes Quick, which appeared to have disintegrated a bit since the post office shut down in 1968, leaving little more than some cleared fields and what appeared, for all intents, to be a jumble of turn-of-the-century roadhouse buildings stitched together under one roof.

The ragged horizon was now clearly comprised of the Telkwa Mountains, which rise from the rolling hill country in the south, and the Skeena Mountains, which rise from the north. After putting in to pick up Rupert-bound travellers at Smithers, the sawmill-and-railroad town that was built almost exclusively on the prosperity this railroad promised, the rail line begins to traverse a landscape, from the moment the train emerges from the shadow of Hudson Bay Mountain, that earned Via Rail's Skeena Run its reputation. The train crisscrossed the westward-flowing Bulkley River on spindly bridges, into a countryside that becomes increasingly tumultuous and chaotic, with distant, solid-rock mountain peaks hovering in the clouds above sprawling farms and ranches along the broad and sweeping Bulkley Valley. As the train moved northwest, it moved through the Wet'suwet'en heartlands, through the centre of the nineteenth-century tribal prophet cults that so perplexed the first Christian missionaries to the area with their accounts of medicine men who visited heaven and returned to earth to prophesy the coming of horses, cattle, and white men.

Winding southwest, the train line twists and turns through cataracts and canyons beneath Mount Rocher Deboule, which is also Stegyawden, with its fabled city of mountain goats, marking the eastern frontier of the Gitksan territories. The open country of spruce and pine turns in on itself under the mountains, becoming a deep and dark forest of hemlock, fir, and cedar, still haunted by the 'watsx, an otterlike being associated with death and madness, and the train crosses the Skeena for the first time near the village of Gitsegukla, on the south bank, where clan chiefs blockaded the river to steamboat traffic in the 1870s after white prospectors burned the village. From there, the line swings from southwest to west, passing through the long-empty Salvation Army village of Andimaul, then slowing down through the village of Gitwangak, where clan chiefs in the 1980s blockaded Via Rail trains over more contemporary grievances, often related to the great bald patches on the mountainsides that seemed to become more frequent with every passing mile.

The train rumbled over the site of Gitwangak's former graveyard, where dozens of box tombs were disinterred to make way for the railroad eighty years earlier. There was a fleeting glimpse of the old heraldic poles for which this village, one of the more ancient Gitksan villages, is known. Gitwangak's standard-issue Indian-reserve houses stand amid old poles that recount innumerable sagas and epics, not the least of which is the Epic of Naeqt, which involves a war between coast tribes and Gitksans that culminated in a gruesome Gitksan victory at an elaborate hilltop fortress, behind the present village, some centuries ago.

The train became noticeably busier with passengers that had come aboard at Burns Lake, Smithers, and New Hazelton. A pair of young Native women sang to their babies in the coach car. The train turned south just beyond Gitwangak, following the Skeena River as it picked up speed and roared along beneath the northern foothills of the Seven Sisters Range in just the same way that Hubert Evans described it in his 1954 novel, *Mist On The River*. In the passage that has young Cy Pitt leaving his home village to make his first trip to work in the canneries on the coast, a tradition that engaged hundreds of Gitksan families in succeeding generations after the first canneries were built on tidewater stilts around Prince Rupert in the late 1800,

> Native people sang on the train going down to the canneries, Cy remembered. And their mother said that before there was a train, in steamboat days, they sang, only then it was mostly the gospel songs. Probably their people sang even in the times before that, when they travelled in the big canoes, when there were no canneries, and no whites, and the country all belonged to native people.

More than anything else, it was this railroad that brought white people into the country, and the railroad was the means, in Hays' grand scheme, to break the CPR's monopoly and turn Vancouver's touted destiny into Prince Rupert's triumph – what with five hundred fewer sea miles between Prince Rupert harbour and the Orient. For Wilfrid Laurier, it meant a great railroad that would be associated with him in the same way that the Canadian Pacific was associated with John A. Macdonald, and, in the bargain, the country's great north country would be thrown open to settlement and the new societies of commerce, religion, and imperialism.

The railroad changed everything, beginning with the place-names on the landscape. A few miles beyond Gitwangak, Mean-skinish – established in the 1880s by Anglican missionary Robert Tomlinson as a village for baptized Gitksans, a refuge from their pagan compatriots – was christened Cedarvale by the Grand Trunk. But the landscape is always changing, Anita Marple pointed out as we passed what was left of Cedarvale. Marple was Via Rail's only female train conductor in Western Canada. One of the changes she meant was how Cedarvale just hadn't been the same since Edith left. Edith Essex, in her nineties, gave up her job as Cedarvale's postmistress in 1994, after serving for seventy years. And there wasn't much left of Doreen, either, another fourteen miles down the line, although Dot Hanson, whose father was a CN section man, still lived there in the bush above what was left of the little town, which was surviving mainly as a place where more urbanized residents of Terrace and Prince Rupert kept their summer cabins. Doreen was still inaccessible by road and completely dependent on the train, so when old Louie died there a few years earlier, it fell to Marple to get off the train and spend the night with Louie's wife, to help her change his clothes and wait with her until the Mounties arrived on a speeder car the following day, when they packed him out, on the train.

And then there was Pacific, which was a bustling little place until the railway division-point moved to Terrace. And then Usk, and then Terrace itself, where Hays' vision was so compelling that a local settler, George Little, donated a seven-acre parcel of land to the Grand Trunk to encourage them to establish a station there. The Grand Trunk did, and named it Littleton, in the settler's honour. But even that didn't last. The postal service didn't want the settlement to get confused with a town of the same name in Ontario, so George Little's place was renamed Terrace.

Beyond Terrace, the train line meanders downriver, punching through tunnel after tunnel until the Skeena grows wider and the mountains fall back and away. The broad river estuary begins at around Kwinitsa, where seagulls hover in the sky and harbour seals glide in the current, and freshwater is overwhelmed on the tides by saltwater at about Haysport, named after Hays himself.

And then the tracks approach Prince Rupert, named in honour of the first governor of the Hudson's Bay Company, a suggestion that won Eleanor MacDonald of Winnipeg a $250 prize, hers being the entry chosen from 12,000 submissions in a contest sponsored by the Grand Trunk Pacific in 1905. All that is left is the final descent, from the Rainbow Bridge along the coast, past the rotting pilings of long-closed canneries, past Sockeye and Phelan and Port Edward and Kaein, to Prince Rupert's old rail yards, below town, 1,058 metres below the height of land at Yellowhead Pass, and the sea.

Finn Slough

At first it was just a lot of talk.

The salmon season had come and gone, Gus Jacobsen's *Eva* was back in her boat shed, and it was just coming on the season of the high winter tides, when even the boardwalk on the island side is floating in the rosehip and the bulrushes. The mergansers had flown south and the occasional goldeneye was showing up. You can tell a goldeneye by the whistle its wings make.

It was the time of year when people up and down Finn Slough start to settle in. They drink tea in front of their woodstoves and look out their windows. The cold southwesterlies blow through the leafless trees from across the river, across Rose Island and Kirkland Island, from Barber Island and Gunn Island. The walls creak in their old wood; the planks and timbers that built these homes were towed in scows from the New Westminster sawmills and hauled here by horse-drawn carts from the old ferry dock more than half a century before.

So there was a lot of talk.

But there had always been a lot of talk about the fate of Finn Slough. It had been that way since the 1920s, and it had never come to much. In the 1930s, city hall tried to push a dyke through Mikko Jacobsen's place without so much as a by-your-leave, so Mikko got an interpreter and fought, and won. All the fishermen celebrated in the new sauna Mikko built over at his place. In the 1940s, there was even an eviction order from Richmond municipal hall, but it turned out to be just talk, and Finn Slough had sustained all kinds of that.

This time, it was supposed to be some developer with big friends and lots of pull at city hall and the harbour commission. But talk like that always came and went, like everything else.

Then there was a notice, and by the look of it, things were probably pretty serious this time. A dozen or so copies of it appeared one morning on bright white sheets of 8½ x 11 paper, tacked on pilings and shed walls all along the boardwalk, up and down the slough. They fluttered and slapped in the wind on the walls of the scow houses, the houseboats, and the old stilt houses that the Finns built before the Spanish Civil War.

Trespassers are required to immediately leave the island.

The notice warned that anyone on the island without the written consent of a company called Smith Prestige Properties Ltd., described only as "the Owner", would be considered a trespasser, and the Owner would take no responsibility for the safety of "trespassers or their belongings". News about Finn Slough's new owner, and the owner's intentions, came to the twenty-odd households along Finn Slough on a Friday, the last day of the last week in November, only six days after Richmond's civic elections had returned a developer's majority of five Non-Partisan Association councillors, a beleaguered Mayor Greg Halsey-Brandt, and a splintered left wing – two Team Richmond candidates and New Democrat Harold Steeves.

Failure to comply will result in court proceedings being initiated with trespassers liable for the court costs attendant in such proceedings.

Among those things that had established Finn Slough in its place here in the world, and for which Smith Prestige Properties Ltd. had declared it would take no responsibility, was an old wood-stave bluestone tank resting in the reeds where it was built in the days when Irish cotton-mill workers made the Fraser's gillnets and the nets had to be treated with bluestone solution so they didn't fall apart. Just downstream of the bluestone tank stood what may have been the only wooden drawbridge left on Canada's West Coast. It was a footbridge across the slough, with planks in the middle that were raised and lowered to let the gillnet boats through to their moorings, which were little more than cradles that stood them upright at low tide. More than half a century had passed since the slough's fishing families joined in and built the bridge with lumber from the Anglo-British Fishing Company cannery. Other belongings included tiny houses, on both sides of the narrow slough, that floated on logs when the tide was high. Some houses rested on stilts embedded in scows that had been sunk long before. Old cedar-shake boat sheds slumped into their pilings, and the whole assemblage was built by men and women with names like Sami Hendrickson, William Haasanen, Mannos Inkstrom, and Matti Lampi, fishermen who left Finland's Gulf of Bothnia in the 1890s for the coal mines of America. Those who did not die from black lung eventually found their way to Canada's West Coast. They were among the first white fishermen on the Fraser River.

There was also Gus Jacobsen's *Eva*, the boat the Kishi brothers built at their Steveston yard for Gus's uncle Henry back in 1939. The *Eva* was still powered by the two-cylinder Easthope that came from the Steveston shop that built the engines that powered the Fraser's gillnet fleet after Gustaf Eldstrom got rid of his gaff-rigged sails one day and put an Easthope in his boat. The other fishermen followed suit.

From its upriver end at Jacobsen's boat shed, Finn Slough's main street, the boardwalk, meandered more or less in a straight line past tidy little plank-walled houses roofed with hand-split shakes. An Indian dip net that washed up one day was hanging on a peg on the wall of what was once a Finnish sauna. Above the door on another shed were red-paint Japanese characters, barely discernible, believed locally to have once warned children to keep out. During the warm nights in the springtime, it was always easier, from this side of the slough, to hear the bellowing and roaring of the California sea lions that arrive for the oolichans every year in herds of hundreds of bachelor bulls. You could hear them especially well from the knoll at the end of the boardwalk, just past the house where Toivo Boren used to live before he left for the Finnish Rest Home back in January 1983 and died five months later, the last of the original Finns who settled here. The knoll was high ground, in a grove of poplar trees, the balm of Gilead kind. In their season, the trees came alive with mourning doves, calliope hummingbirds, and woodpeckers. The kind of trees that Matti Lampi used to climb every afternoon, like clockwork, to call his pigs from the fields.

In those earlier days, too, in their season, the sea lions bellowed and roared. And just as it was in those earlier days, there were rough-legged hawks, sharp-shinned hawks, and Cooper's hawks. There were snipes, juncos, and trumpeting clouds of snow geese from Siberia that you could hear from those little houses just as clearly as in the days when the women knitted sweaters with wool from sheep they raised in the nearby fields and talked about the latest news from newspapers with names like *Vapaus*, which means Freedom, and *Liekki*, which means Flame. It was in these same houses that Kalle Huovinen, Ensti Tuorela, and the others sat at tables and deliberated late into the night and decided, in the end, to charter the Finn Slough fishermen into the One Big Union, the union of Joe Hill, Ginger Goodwin, and the Everett martyrs.

What was not so easy to establish in any kind of ordered inventory was the impact Smith Prestige Properties Ltd.'s November notices had within the latter-day households of Finn Slough, among those people who persisted in living here despite the uncertain tenure, the worrisome storms, and the absence of covered parking and vinyl siding. People like Brent McKay, who would sometimes find himself on the streets of Richmond, looking around and asking himself where everything had gone. Or Dinny Lansdowne, who worked on a salmon seiner for eleven years before deciding to quit but couldn't bring herself to be away from the water, so she moved into a house that floated at high tide. Or Jim Munro, who was born and raised in Steveston but didn't feel at all at home there anymore and insisted that the fate of Finn Slough was not just a municipal issue, it was a national issue, if for no other reason than the fact that the slough had probably been painted, sketched for postcards, and photographed as much as any other place with boats this side of Peggy's Cove. Or David Dorrington, who said it was the fact that people continued to live in Finn Slough that had assured its protection and that it was one of the few examples anywhere in the Lower Mainland of people actually living in some harmony within the natural environment. Or Nadeane Trowse, who finally found her way here from Prince George after deciding that this was the place she wanted to live when she read about the slough in a book of poetry by Daphne Marlatt. That was in 1973.

So, after Smith Prestige Properties Ltd. posted its NO TRESPASSING signs and later attempted to persuade the local Canada Post letter carrier to divulge the precise addresses of the Finn Slough residents who used the rural-route postbox up on River Road, the slough's residents set up their own community association and posted their own notices, addressed to Smith Prestige Properties Ltd., on the boardwalk posts and at the footbridge.

> All structures that are on the foreshore between high and low tide are on Crown land. If any person causes damage to persons or property on Crown land at Finn Slough, action will be taken to the fullest extent of the law by the Finn Slough Heritage and Wetland Society.

So you could say the lines were drawn. But as uncertain as things might have seemed that November, they were still a lot clearer than the world looks through a north-south grid map of property lines that had been imposed on the estuary of the Fraser River after the first pre-emption laws came into effect in the 1800s. The river doesn't run in such neat, straight lines. The landscape tends to change as quickly as the companies that purport to own the land, and sometimes the land just disappears and reappears somewhere else. As far as anyone at Finn Slough could determine, they didn't even live on private land, so how could they be evicted by a private-property owner?

Over the years, the slough itself was the only thing that had been in any way constant. You could say that much, but even that was not completely true, because Finn Slough's significance as a waterway on any given day might depend on the phase of the moon, the snowpack on the mountains far in the Interior the previous winter, the seasons, and the wind from the Gulf, and the slough had been a much more significant waterway before the upriver side silted up sometime around 1960. Finn Island used to be called Anderson Island, and the latest deeds were calling it Whitworth Island. On the marine charts it was Gilmour Island, but some Richmond street maps had it as Woodward Island. The first Crown grant was in 1875, but that was when the main channel of the river ran past Ladner, and the river outside Finn Slough and Steveston was just a murky and fog-ridden warren of side channels and marsh. The Crown grant awarded a pre-emption of Section 22, Block 3 to one Henry Valentino Edwards, who sold it to John Roland Hett the following year, who appears to have flipped it a few days later to John Ross Foord. Then there was the 1898 flood. Then came the 1948 flood, and by then what had been a thirty-eight-acre potato farm was reduced to a five-acre parcel, most of which was woods and marsh, and all of it was inundated in the spring freshets and below the high-tide line in winter anyway. For a time in the 1980s it was owned by Sceptre Dredging, and then Roy Dales, and in 1989 he sold it. Sometime later it showed up as the property of Smith Prestige Properties Ltd.

Placing Finn Slough's purported owners and their intentions in any sort of orderly arrangement proved every bit as difficult. A company named Smith Prestige Properties Ltd. appeared to hold fee-simple title to something in the area, at least. The company's lawyers were fielding its calls, and the company itself seemed to be the possession of two Ontario residents, Stephen Smith and James Sebastian. But calls about Smith Prestige Properties Ltd.'s Richmond holding were handled by Walt Johnson, a consultant, and big-time developers Aplan-Martin and Associates were involved in the whole thing, too. Aplan-Martin was an outfit with lots of Richmond development experience behind it. Johnson described himself as a "major player" in huge suburban real-estate developments such as Coquitlam's Westwood Plateau and the River Heights developments and the Blair Rifle Range. While the plans for Finn Slough were taking shape, another Johnson client, Tripower Development, was in the process of evicting marine tenants on the river side of the dyke adjoining a Queensborough subdivision development a few miles upriver from Finn Slough. Johnson agreed that all of this should make an interesting story, except that the way he would have told it, it would have been a story about taxes. These people lived in what might be described as houses, in what might be described as Richmond, but they did not pay property taxes. Technically, although these individuals did not reside on land, as such, they did reside on the property of a taxpaying property owner – Smith Prestige Properties Ltd. – which intended to develop the property even though thirty-three of its thirty-eight acres were underwater and the five remaining acres were only above water some of the time, and despite the fact that it was all within the Department of Fisheries and Oceans' no-development "red zone".

The company was considering a number of options. One of them was a modern floating-home development (an option Johnson said he didn't prefer). The company had won "unofficial approval" from the multi-bureaucracy Fraser River Estuary Management Program and from municipal officials, and there was talk about a land swap – Richmond would get some parkland and the company would get more real estate or a special deal somewhere else, but the company would also get an access road connecting Number Four and Number Five roads for its development at or in or around Finn Slough.

As for Gus Jacobsen, Brent McKay, Dinny Lansdowne, Jim Munro, David Dorrington, Nadeane Trowse, and the rest, the role they would play in Johnson's telling of the story would be that of a dangerous liability for Richmond, a collection of households with no adequate fire protection, no sewage system, and a dubious water supply. They were "squatters". Johnson noted that the municipal elections had just come and gone and it would be three years until the next one, so now was the time to move. He was preparing a questionnaire for distribution among two hundred area residents who, he said, would be "flabbergasted" to learn that Finn Slough's households owned no land, paid no taxes, had no sewage system, and that among them was a professor from the University of British Columbia who was earning his wages from public funds and was probably the power behind all the "negativism" coming from the slough. The upshot of all this should be a compromise, Johnson proposed. Smith Prestige would be able to act with the liberty of any property owner. The government could declare the place a park or a heritage site as long as Smith Prestige got compensated. But Smith Prestige owned the place and, after all, Smith Prestige paid taxes.

As for taxes, Walt Johnson did not appear to hold the view that ill-planned subdivision development from Garry Point to Abbotsford had already drained countless millions of dollars

from taxpayers throughout the province through the 1980s and
1990s, all to pay for roads, bridges, and other infrastructure sub-
sidies to the Lower Mainland's real-estate industry. Richmond
alone had come to be served by four major bridges, a tunnel, a
freeway, an elaborate freeway-connection system to the sprawling subdivisions on the route out to the Alex Fraser Bridge, and
two minor bridges, one of which was built in 1991 to provide
access to a cluster of subdivisions south of the Middle Arm that
should never have been built in the first place. Richmond's population was growing at a rate exceeding five percent every year,
and to build places for all these commuters to watch television
before they fell asleep, the municipality had buried its few
remaining berry bogs and knocked down what little forest
remained on the eastern end of the island. It continued to pour
sewage through out-of-date primary-treatment centres into the
Fraser, the river that gave Richmond its birth. The whole place,
in just a few years, had become little more than an assemblage of
mini-malls and monster houses, with little to show for itself,
apart from various monuments to Hong Kong capital like the
Aberdeen Mall and the Yoahan Centre, for all its tireless suck-
ing-up to the real-estate industry. Which was now turning its
attentions to Finn Slough.

"It's gone to hell," was the way Gus Jacobsen described the
situation.

Gus was born in 1939, the year his gillnetter, the *Eva*, was
built. Down through the years, while the rest of the salmon boats
were constantly upgrading and remaking themselves, the *Eva*
continued to fish the Fraser with its two-cylinder Easthope, until
it was one of the few Easthopes that remained in the fleet. The
Eva had replaced the *Ina*, powered by a single-cylinder Easthope,
about which all Gus would say was, "She is no longer." If you

asked Gus Jacobsen what he meant when he said that Richmond had gone to hell, he would tell you that every year he used to kill two thousand barn rats, and that's because you've got to kill a barn rat before you kill a muskrat, because barn rats come out about an hour earlier than a muskrat does and muskrat pelts paid his way through school. Muskrat, otter, and coon formed the staple of his trapline, which had long been covered over by subdivisions. He started fishing when he was ten, got his first hunting licence when he was eleven, and what Gus Jacobsen saw when he looked around was not what Walt Johnson saw. What Jacobsen saw, in his own words, was "Richmond falling apart", and if Finn Slough was going to go, nobody would be able to replace it. Not for any amount of money.

And as far as taxes went, Finn Slough had heard it all before. Gus Jacobsen was a direct descendant of Mikko Hihnala, who was born in 1850 in the village of Himanka, Finland, and ended up building a scow house for himself on the Fraser, near what became the foot of Number Three Road, in 1892. Mikko Hihnala was the first of the Richmond Finns. Others followed and joined him, and they remained in their floating village until 1927, when they were threatened with eviction – for not paying taxes. Taxes were what caused the Finns to move about a half-kilometre downstream and pull their scow houses up into the slough that came to bear their name. The Finn Slough Heritage and Wetland Society was prepared to come to terms with things like taxes.

After November's NO TRESPASSING signs went up, Finn Slough's households spent the winter heading off the sewage argument by building composting toilets, putting them well ahead of Richmond's subdivisions, which still relied on outdated sewage-treatment plants. As winter turned to spring, the Finn Slough households discussed how to buy their way into the land-side legitimacy of property ownership, but they couldn't bring themselves to agree that they lived on land, and they didn't relish the idea of shelling out money without some security of tenure in return. As for Walt Johnson's tip about a sinister university professor behind all the trouble, no such culprit could be found. Among the residents and occupants of Finn Slough were a set designer, a senior federal administrator, a marine engineer, a shipwright, a mother, a musician, a writer, a boat skipper, a sculptor, a graduate student, a contractor, a designer, a recreation-management worker, five fishermen, a marine surveyor, a teacher, a park-board employee, and a millwork-shop owner. Average length of residency: twelve years. There were more than fifty of them, and they vowed to stay put and that was all there was to that. They were determined to stay. They had sisu.

Sisu is a word that is as difficult to translate from the Finnish as it is to translate the value of places like Finn Slough into the kind of language that is comprehensible in the proceedings of advisory planning committees, boards of variance, municipal zoning hearings, or any of those places where the dismemberment and burial of so many of the lower Fraser's maritime villages had been decided over the years. The way Eric Sorila translated it, sisu means stamina. Sisu means obstinate perseverance. It is what had allowed the Finns to survive out there on the southern shore of Lulu Island, outside the dykes, in the marsh, in an environment that is as much land as water, and as much ocean as river. Sisu is what had allowed them to prevail for so long against the combined weight of nickel-a-fish cannery prices, petty civic bureaucrats, a hostile Anglo-Saxon ascendancy, and the schemes of real-estate speculators. A quarter century had passed since Eric Sorila first visited Finn Slough. It took Sorila fifteen years of patience before he managed to buy a vacant house in the slough, which had become a place of ancestral significance for B.C.'s Finnish community, as much as Sointula, and of the same meaning that Gimli is to Icelanders, Paldi is to Sikhs, and Krestova is to the Sons of Freedom. Sorila was luckier than many. It was not often that such a chance would come along, when someone pulled up stakes and sold an old Finn Slough scow house. So Sorila bided his time.

Sisu.

On a rainy day in Brent McKay's tiny living room, more than a dozen neighbours gathered around the woodstove to talk about whatever it was they were finding themselves up against. The room was quiet when Eric Sorila was talking. Sorila was the slough's historian and chronicler, the community's department of vital statistics and its land-registry office, and there were likely very few people who had ever passed through the place whose names and life struggles were not known to Sorila, a photographer and vice-president of the British Columbia Finnish Heritage Society. In his hand, Sorila held a green bottle. He had found it almost a metre deep in the mud, when he was digging up a telephone cable. By its markings, he reckoned it was about seventy years old. Embedded in the glass: "Vat 69 Scotch Whiskey". The cork was still in it. The bottle had never been opened. "People were born here," Sorila said. "People were brought up here. It's a piece of history that's very unique in Canada. It's part of our life, and if the developers have their way, it will be buried in the sand. And that is just too horrendous to think about."

Terra Nova was already buried in the sand beneath the condominiums on the far side of Lulu Island from Finn Slough. Terra Nova had been settled in the 1890s by Newfoundlanders who farmed the boggy ground and fished for the Terra Nova and Alliance canneries. In 1981, when the provincial heritage conservation branch completed an exhaustive review of the lower Fraser area – called the Fraser Estuary Heritage Resource Inventory – the branch recommended that Terra Nova's farming character be maintained and its remaining buildings protected. Before the 1980s were over, Richmond municipal council saw to it that Terra Nova was ploughed under. By then, old Steveston was all but gone, and what remained survived as a backdrop to what was becoming more of a Steveston-theme mall than anything else. On the North Arm's south shore, Eburne was a thriving community shortly after Harry Eburne opened his general store there in the 1880s. Grauer's Store closed in 1976 after more than sixty years of business. In the weeks before the heritage inventory was released, the last of Eburne's buildings were bulldozed. Across the river from Eburne, the 1897 Celtic cannery and shipyard remained only for as long as it took a condominium developer to propose that the site be obliterated. Less than five years after the heritage resource inventory recommended that the Celtic site be preserved, the bustling little shipyard was gone. The 1981 inventory said this about Finn Slough: "It is strongly recommended that this heritage area be retained as it presently exists. The fishing community is an important element in the heritage of the Fraser estuary. This area should remain publicly accessible."

The inventory's authors said the same kind of thing about the Pacific Coast Terminals' clock tower, which had loomed over the river at New Westminster since the days of grain ships bound for Shanghai in the 1930s. It said the same kind of thing about the B.C. Penitentiary's wardens' residences, the site of the old Hawaiian settlement at Kanaka Creek, Little Norway on the Pitt River,

Port Mann on the Fraser, Saint Mungo's at Sunbury, and Ladner's Chinatown, where cannery hands smoked opium, dreamed
of home in Canton, and died of malnutrition and typhoid fever
between the sockeye seasons. Where Chung Chuck, the potato
grower who would not back down to anybody, found himself up
against bylaw-enforcement officers trying to shut down his door-
to-door potato truck business. He chased them off with two-by-
fours. Years later, he stared down a police tactical squad that
arrived with municipal crews to shut off his water and drive out
his old houseboat colony. There were flashing red lights and there
was a frail old man coming out from between the trees. He raised
his rifle to his shoulder and stood his ground like the old days: I
grow potato. I sell potato.

Sisu.

The 1981 Fraser River Estuary Heritage Inventory was more
than 250 pages long. Finn Slough was just one entry, on one
page. The inventory was published less than fifteen years before
Smith Prestige Properties Ltd. posted its 8½ x 11 NO TRESPASS-
ING signs on Finn Slough's boat sheds and scow houses, but by
that November morning it no longer served as a useful inventory
of important places that should be respected and left alone.
Instead, it served only as a catalogue of all those people, and all
those places, that we had lost.

But we had not lost Finn Slough.

Three years after all the talk that November, Smith Prestige
Properties Ltd. was still claiming to have serious plans to build
250 townhouses on dredged landfill that would cover Finn
Slough and jut straight out into the river's navigation channel.
Nobody from the slough had any plans to give up, and the Finn
Slough Wetlands and Preservation Society was standing firm in
its vow that its people were staying put. There had been lots of

meetings with Smith Prestige and lots of meetings with the harbour commission. Finn Slough's households were told they would have to come up with a full community plan, complete with architectural guidelines and legal descriptions, in order to "regularize" themselves. McKay, Lansdowne, Munro, and the others found it would cost them about $12,000. They raised the $12,000. There were more meetings planned, and Smith Prestige was still talking about all the compensation it would be owed for such a lost business opportunity.

The *Eva* was lost to the commercial salmon fleet in 1996. It was an old boat, no match for the aluminum diesel boats and high-speed bowpickers the gillnet fleet was turning to, so Gus Jacobsen sold his fishing licence. All the old canneries were shut down for good, but the *Eva* remained at her moorings in Finn Slough, and sometimes, when the river was quiet, Gus would warm her up, take her out on the slack tide, and put her through her paces.

From far off, there was no mistaking the sound of the *Eva* with her old two-cylinder Easthope. It ran like a charm.

From the Old Rice Mill to Annieville Drift

Looking out my front window up the channel, I could see all the gillnet boats were still tied to their moorings. Another night had passed and the boats hadn't gone fishing. The *Joy-Ethel*, the *Slo-Poke*, the *Panther*, the *Escorial*, and the *Three Sons* rolled gently in the wind. It was the last week of July, 1992. It was raining.

What I remember about those days is that there had been a lot of herons around, and more seals than usual. And there was a kingfisher that had taken to perching on top of one of the old pilings by the railway into the Manucks' boat shed. It was there for days, diving into the shallow water, gorging itself on the pink-salmon fry that were clinging to the shore on their way down-river to the sea.

Millions of pink salmon had passed upriver the year before. You could see them jumping all over Annacis Channel, all along the south shore of Queensborough up to New Westminster's waterfront, day after day. The river had been thick with them, but the companies didn't want to pay the union fishermen the contract minimum for pinks. There were so many fish, there was no margin in it. Some of my neighbours petitioned for a food fishery at least, like the Indians had, but the fisheries department said no. So by the last days of July, 1992, the mud banks of the Fraser River all along Annacis Channel swarmed with the off-spring of that pink run, on their way to the sea. They schooled in dark clouds just beneath the surface. They swarmed between the long legs of fishing herons, and the kingfisher fell upon them from its perch outside my window.

Out in the channel and in the deeper main-stem reaches, from the old rice mill to Annieville drift, other ancient cycles were at work. Sockeye, the big-money fish, were moving upriver, but it was nothing like the pink-salmon run the year before. For one thing, 1992's Fraser River runs were on the lowest year of the sockeye's four-year cycle. Nobody's quite sure why Fraser sock-eye return in these dominant, subdominant, and low-year runs, but that's the way the sockeye cycle on the Fraser has worked for as long as anybody seems to know. Still, there had been two days' sockeye fishing earlier in the season, and there had been more openings planned. Every day, the fishermen would wait to hear word from the fisheries department about when they could go out. Every day, Wayne Crawford, Barry and Vince Manuck, the Petrunia brothers, and all the other Queensborough gillnet-ters waited for some news. Now and then a Musqueam skiff would pass down the channel and everybody along the slough would stop what they were doing and just watch the Indians go by. One day passed into the next.

From my houseboat window, overlooking the gillnet boats along Annacis Channel, all I knew was that the sockeye were moving upriver to the Nadina, the Gates, the Chilko, the Stellako, and the hundreds of small rivers and streams throughout the Interior. Most of the sockeye runs had already passed, my neighbours weren't fishing, and none of them knew why.

At the time, I was still employed as a senior reporter for the *Vancouver Sun*. The paper had recently taken on yet another "new look", concerned mainly with the affairs of the Lower Mainland's booming suburbs. The *Sun* had recently eliminated its forestry beat, its Native-affairs beat, its fisheries beat, and its multiculturalism beat. The environment beat was barely there. The weekend editions carried a prominent section called "New Homes", a real-estate supplement advertising the kind of subdivisions that were poised to bury Finn Slough and were already being built on top of Queensborough and Ladner and Annieville and Port Guichon and Sunbury, leaving fishermen like my neighbours in Annacis Channel clinging to the edge of the river side of the dyke while city-council members uptown complained about the eyesores their boat sheds had become. Something was happening, but nobody knew what it was. July turned to August, and the fishermen waited for news.

When it came, what they were presented with was the first volley in a bizarre eruption of panic and fear that ended up shaking the British Columbia coast. It infected the schoolrooms in Campbell River, the bars in Prince Rupert, and the malls in Port Alberni. What British Columbians were to be served up on an almost daily basis in their newspapers, on the radio, and in television broadcasts had about as much to do with the facts as what we were told about Japanese fishermen's ham-radio transmissions to enemy ships offshore back in 1941. A half-century later, we were being led to believe that the West Coast's vast fisheries resources were being secretly transferred to Indians according to a diabolical master plan developed in Ottawa. The scare stories were typified by a newspaper advertisement bought by the B.C. Fisheries Survival Coalition, the main front group that had sprung up over the "Native issue". The advertisement told us: "Federal politicians have now decreed that the colour of your skin will determine whether you can earn a living in Canada's multi-billion-dollar fishing industries." On an almost daily basis, we were being told to brace ourselves for the plunder of fisheries, wildlife, timber, and other natural resources as Indians forwarded a hidden agenda to obtain "special rights" for themselves, "rights based on race". A climate of hysteria prevailed throughout the coast, like dirty weather, and it was manufactured by the same coastal fishing companies that had maintained a monopoly over British Columbia's fisheries since the 1800s. In the 1990s, it was the menace of Native fishing rights. The sky was falling again.

At first there were just rumours, traded up and down the lower reaches of the Fraser River, at coffee shops and in dockside chatter from Port Hammond to Port Guichon. Upriver, the Indians were fishing twenty-four hours a day. Nets were strung bank to bank. You couldn't put a boat in up above Chilliwack without getting your outboard fouled. Indians from Alberta and Saskatchewan and Washington state were pouring down into the Fraser Canyon. Freezer trucks filled with sockeye were heading south at night across the border at Sumas, and that's why there was no fishing. The government was giving it all away to the Indians. At first, there was nothing on television, nothing in the newspapers. It was all rumour. Every day, I'd call city desk. Every day, the word was the same: "The newspaper isn't interested in fish anymore."

I made a few calls of my own upriver. It was true there had been problems, and there was a lot of confusion. Things were different in 1992 – it had been two years since the Supreme Court of Canada, in what came to be known as the "Sparrow decision", upheld a century's worth of Native arguments about their fishing rights. The judges ruled that Canada's Constitution protected those rights. Because federal law has to be consistent with the Constitution, it meant big changes. The change came in Ottawa's "Aboriginal Fisheries Strategy". It was billed as an attempt to build a new regime in the Department of Fisheries and Oceans' relations with Indians, and 1992 was its first year of operation.

There was still a wide gulf between perception and reality about what the Sparrow decision was all about, but what the decision meant was that Ottawa couldn't simply boss Indians around anymore when it came to tribal fisheries, which the judges described as fisheries for "food, social, and ceremonial purposes" that could be undertaken "in a contemporary manner". The judges didn't try to be explicit in defining fishing rights. The judges did say, though, that Ottawa had to turn to "the Aboriginal perspective itself on the meaning of the rights at stake". Instead of setting out some kind of inventory of fishing rights, the judges opted to impose what they called "a measure of control over government conduct and a strong check on legislative power". That meant that Ottawa had to justify any measures that might interfere with tribal fisheries, and they couldn't close the river to Native fishing unless there was a "valid" reason, like a legitimate conservation objective. All this posed a particular difficulty for fisheries management because although the tribal fisheries were supposed to have priority in planning, the tribal fisheries took place mainly in the river systems, so they were always the last to go fishing. That meant Ottawa would have to reach agreements with tribal groups about allocations, quotas, fishing times, enforcement, and things like that long before the season began. In one of those agreements, Natives from twenty-three bands from Musqueam to the Fraser Canyon were selling their fish openly for the first time after decades of black-marketing portions of their "food fish" catch, and the coastal canning monopoly was furious. Mike Hunter, president of the Fisheries Council of B.C., complained: "Everywhere we turn, control is being given to the Indians."

There was some truth to the rumours about how all the fisheries officers seemed to have disappeared, particularly upstream, above the canyon, where some officers had been reassigned to other duties and there was less of an enforcement presence than usual. From the canyon on downstream there was a lot of confusion, because the Aboriginal Fisheries Strategy agreement with lower Fraser Natives had been cobbled together at the last minute and because there were a lot more people than usual out fishing, but all ninety-seven bands throughout the Fraser River system were fishing within their pre-Sparrow allocations (the aboriginal fisheries' share of the coast-wide salmon catch in 1992 was about five percent, and four years later, it was still about five percent). Nobody was catching all that much anyway.

And then it happened. On August 21, the Fisheries Council of B.C. – the industry lobby representing B.C. Packers, the Canadian Fishing Company, J. S. McMillan, Ocean Fisheries, and a few more – went to B.C. Supreme Court and asked for an injunction to scuttle the agreements under the Aboriginal Fisheries Strategy that allowed lower Fraser Natives to sell the fish they caught. Between them, those companies – with the multinational food conglomerate Weston Foods tied in as a key parent company – accounted for almost the entire production and distribution of B.C. salmon products. They came to court arm in arm with the Pacific Fishermen's Alliance – the named plaintiff in the case – and with the B.C. Wildlife Federation, the Steelhead Society of British Columbia, and the United Fishermen and Allied Workers Union. Their lawyers submitted affidavits containing a terrifying scenario – an ecological cataclysm had occurred in the Fraser River. They claimed that 1.2 million Fraser River sockeye had "disappeared" between Mission Bridge and their spawning grounds. Indian poachers were to blame.

They had hired a couple of would-be private detectives to spy on Native fishermen all summer, and all those dockside rumours had come mainly from their cloak-and-dagger work in the canyon. They presented the court with a series of affidavits. Retired Mountie Ken Conrad, one of the fishing companies' investigators, reported that he bought a fish in Ladner from an individual who told him the fish was caught the previous day – when the tribal fisheries were closed. He also reported seeing Natives fishing July 26 in the Yale area, during a closure. (It turned out that what he had observed was a legal fishery; the Yale band fishery was open.) The other detective was Bill Wimpney, a B.C. Wildlife Federation spokesman who described himself as a "retired serviceman" (he later went on to become an organizer for the Reform party). Wimpney swore affidavits containing eyewitness reports, sometimes of perfectly legal activity, sometimes of Natives fishing during closures, and sometimes just of improperly marked nets. It was all pretty standard stuff. Most were routine infractions, and many if not all of the incidents were known to federal fisheries officers who were proceeding with their investigations with the support of Sto:lo chiefs. In the end, the plaintiffs had little evidence to show for their efforts, and the judge tossed the case out of court. But one thing the plaintiffs did have was videotape of Indians fishing. It was film the six o'clock news could broadcast. What was useless to them in court was useful enough to ensure that the most outrageous of their allegations eventually found their way into front-page headlines and BCTV *Newshour* horror stories. In all the mayhem that followed, what was missed was the facts, and what went unremarked was the agenda behind the Pacific Fishermen's Alliance in B.C. Supreme Court that day.

The real quarry was aboriginal rights, and August 21, 1992, wasn't the first time the Alliance had raised the spectre of an ecological disaster in its arguments. Two years earlier, Alliance lawyer Chris Harvey warned concerned fishermen at a Richmond meeting that a "back-to-the-jungle free-for-all" would result if Indians gained any control over their fisheries. Long condemned by the church-based Project North as a racist organization, the Alliance became a darling of the downtown media. The Alliance had been at its crusades since at least 1986, when it scored an injunction that scuttled then-Indian Affairs Minister David Crombie's approval of Gitksan band bylaws allowing the sale of fish outside the coastal monopoly's control. The Fisheries Council's Mike Hunter had long before declared aboriginal fishing rights to be "obnoxious, invalid, and un-Canadian", and the Alliance's clarion call to white fishermen was spelled out clearly in a 1991 newsletter: "If the aboriginal right to fish is allowed, economic ruin will result." From 1986 to 1990, the Alliance and the Fisheries Council had fought against the Sparrow case from the B.C. Court of Appeal to the Supreme Court of Canada, and they lost miserably. In 1987, the Alliance tried to persuade the courts to scuttle the twelve years of land-claims talks between Ottawa and the Nisga'a people of the Nass Valley. The Alliance failed in that action, too, but the hysteria their actions provoked persuaded federal negotiators to back away from a Nisga'a fisheries agreement.

When the rule of law fails, there's always mob rule, and on the Fraser River, news about the injunction application swept upstream like a tidal wave. It was just as well that the Musqueam skiffs weren't making their way down Annacis Channel after that. Within weeks, commercial fishermen were descending in their hundreds on downtown streets and rafting their boats together in harbour protests from Prince Rupert to Vancouver. The Fisheries Council's Hunter was telling anyone who would listen that Indian overfishing had caused a "major environmental crisis" on the Fraser River. Dennis Brown of the fishermen's union weighed in with his version of events, calling it a "real biological disaster".

The *Sun* did send a reporter upriver eventually, but he didn't have much to report except rumours about what had been going on and Indians complaining that whoever got all the fish, it sure wasn't them. All the public was told was that 1.2 million fish had somehow "disappeared" in the Native fisheries. That's the story the fishing companies wanted out there, and that's the story they got. Sometimes it was 1.2 million, sometimes it was "between 500,000 and one million", sometimes it was just 500,000. But it was always "the case of the missing fish", and the culprits were always the same. The Indians.

In September 1992, I took a leave of absence from the *Sun* to follow up on an offer from Ernie Crey, fisheries manager for the Lower Fraser Fishing Authority, to investigate each and every allegation about Native poaching on the Fraser River that year and to try to piece together the big picture. At the time, I figured there was probably a lot of truth to all the rumours, and the deal was that if I was going to go poking around upriver, there would have to be no conditions. That was the deal, and the Lower Fraser Fishing Authority was clearly the best place to start looking. The LFFA was the tribal alliance for twenty-three Indian bands from the Fraser Canyon to the mouth of the river – twenty-one Sto:lo bands and the Musqueam and Tsawwassen. These were the Natives most often cited as the main culprits behind the "missing sockeye". These were the Natives who had fought for decades for the right to sell the fish they caught – the way they'd sold fish into world markets through Hawaii to the tune of nine thousand barrels of salted salmon a year between 1846 and 1859. The way they'd sold fish to the Hudson's Bay Company sixty years before the cannery-instigated "food-fish only" rules were implemented by Ottawa in 1888, locking them into poverty. From then on, the "food-fish" rules made a captive labour pool out of the Native fishermen on the coast. If they wanted to continue to fish commercially, they had to get a licence, and back then it was the canneries that issued the licences. Some Native communities did their best to adapt, and over the years there were individual Native fishermen who prospered and ended up as successful fishermen in the coastal salmon fisheries. But the Sto:lo were hit hard. In their territory, no commercial fishing of any kind was allowed – Mission was the upriver extent of commercial fishing. So down through the decades, the Sto:lo practised their own ways of making the best of a bad situation, turning black-market fish sales into a respected and highly disciplined art form. It was the Sto:lo, the Musqueam, and the Tsawwassen – along with the Nuu-Chah-Nulth on Vancouver Island's west coast and the Skeena River First Nations – whose insistence on restoring commercial components of their tribal fisheries in 1992 represented such an unacceptable impertinence to the canning-industry monopoly.

I spent two months on the LFFA investigation, and I agreed to stick around over the winter and help out with the LFFA's own community review of 1992's fisheries. I talked to fishermen from Skawahlook to Kwakwawapilt and from Chawathil to Chehalis. We managed to get hold of the field notes of the self-styled secret agents the fishing companies had hired to spy on Indians all summer, and we checked out every allegation. I interviewed fisheries officers and area residents. I filled almost a dozen notebooks, working closely with the LFFA's own fisheries guardians and Department of Fisheries and Oceans field staff. I interviewed old-time black-market buyers at the back of low-rent restaurants in Whalley and pored over exotic catch-per-unit-of-effort statistics from the Fraser Canyon with the LFFA's patient biologists.

It's true that there were problems with enforcement. Most of the problems seemed to stem from the fact that the snail's-pace federal bureaucracy produced an eleventh-hour agreement stitched together just as the fish were entering the river. It's true that there were a lot more nets in the river than usual, and nobody was annoyed by this more than the longtime Sto:lo fishermen themselves. Some people were still sneaking around at night selling their fish as though nothing had changed since the bad old days. Fisheries enforcement staff were confused about exactly what they could do, given the tremendous constraints placed on them by the Sparrow decision, and their bosses didn't have many answers either. The DFO field officers who wanted to take charge had the support of the key Sto:lo chiefs, like Tzeachten's Kenny Malloway and Cheam's Sam Douglas, but often the local DFO staff didn't have the resources (at one point they had to ask the LFFA for gas money for their patrol boats). In spite of all this,

senior DFO enforcement officers like Wayne Furness and Elliott
Teske kept telling me they'd seen better compliance in the Sto:lo
territories in 1992 than in any year in their careers.

The weeks were passing, and the numbers weren't adding up.
If 1.2 million fish had "gone missing" in the river as they made
their way home to the spawning grounds, somewhere upstream
of Mission Bridge, where could it have happened? How could it
have happened? By October, what had become obvious was that
we were looking in the wrong places all along. Sure, there were
problems in the river. There was "poaching". Upriver of the
LFFA area, there was virtually no catch-monitoring to speak of.
And there were dead, diseased-looking fish floating downstream
all summer. But there was clearly something else at work.

What became obvious soon enough was that while everybody
was focusing on what was going on in the river, the real story
was to be found in the sequence of fisheries-planning decisions
and in boardrooms in Ottawa and in Washington, D.C., where
negotiations had failed to produce a renewal of the Canada-U.S.
salmon treaty – the protocol that sets the rules governing how
many Fraser-bound salmon U.S. fishermen can catch. It's too
simple to say "the fish never got to the river" and leave it at that.
But the fact is that while my neighbours were waiting to be told
when they could set their nets, dozens of massive seine boats
were out in the Juan de Fuca Strait, fishing night and day.

Most of the seine fleet is owned or otherwise controlled by the
big companies affiliated with the Fisheries Council of B.C., and
while the Fisheries Council was preparing for its August 21
courtroom publicity stunt, fisheries biologists down at the
Department of Fisheries and Oceans' headquarters in Vancouver
were trying to assess the damage that resulted from the collapse
of negotiations for a renewal of the Canada-U.S. salmon treaty.

While Conrad and Wimpney were spying on Native fishermen from behind trees near Spuzzum, the DFO biologists in Vancouver had been busy purging from their computer screens the Canadian seine fleet's preseason sockeye catch limits. Out in Juan de Fuca, the seine skippers got the word over their radios. They were being told to go ahead and fish until their nets came up empty. The new plan was to allow the big-boat seine fleet to catch as many sockeye as possible before the fish started swimming through American waters. It was an old-fashioned fish war.

If there were any winners in the war, they were among the Fisheries Council's affiliates. The Weston company alone could account for fully fifty percent of all the Fraser-bound sockeye in some years. The companies had gone with the flow of free trade (North American Free Trade Agreement negotiator Simon Reisman was a Weston company board member), opening lower-wage plants in Washington and Alaska, and the Fisheries Council companies' supply was secured in the main through their ownership and control of the salmon fleet, mainly the seine boats. There were about five hundred seine boats in the fleet in 1992, and those five hundred boats were catching about half the sockeye and pink salmon on B.C.'s coast. The four thousand gill-netters and trollers in the small-boat fleet were left to fight over the rest, and they were still obliged to sell most of their fish to the Fisheries Council companies. The companies had cornered production years earlier, and some of them had invested heavily in fish farms to ease their reliance on fishermen and wild salmon. Almost all the Native commercial fishermen on the coast were still beholden to them in one way or another, and more than a fifth of the fishermen feeding their canning lines were Natives. The companies had vowed more than once that there was no way a bunch of backwoods Indian chiefs were going to change arrangements like that. "People will not stand for it," the Alliance's Paddy Greene warned. More than $1 billion in capital investments were involved in the commercial fishery, and "a financial disaster for Canadians of every race" would surely result from all this talk about tribal fisheries and cottage industries and communal rights.

As the Fraser-bound sockeye made their way down Vancouver Island's west coast in the summer of 1992, the companies' seine fleet hit hard. The Canadian seiners took 400,000 sockeye over and above their preseason allocations. The sockeye, not knowing where the U.S. border transects Juan de Fuca Strait, swam into the nets of U.S. fishermen, who caught 320,000 sockeye more than they would have caught under the treaty. Before the outside fleets were finished, almost 3.5 million Fraser River sockeye had been caught before they reached the river – the biggest commercial bonanza on that cycle year in fifty years. The end result was that not enough sockeye entered the mouth of the river to satisfy spawning goals, the allocations to aboriginal fisheries, and the fisheries my neighbours were waiting for. That's why my neighbours were on the beach. That's why they couldn't go fishing. And just when they started to scream about being shut out of the river, the Fisheries Council and its Pacific Fishermen's Alliance arrived on August 21 with all the simple answers: it was a "back to the jungle" fishery upriver, and the Indians caught all the fish.

The twenty-three LFFA Indian bands hadn't been fishing since August 19. Something was wrong in the river. The alarm bells sounded, and the Sto:lo didn't go fishing again. Fisheries Minister John Crosbie took a while to respond, but when he did, he vowed to leave no question unanswered. He assigned resource economist Peter Pearse and fisheries scientist Peter Larkin, a Rhodes scholar and professor emeritus at the University of B.C., to conduct the federal investigation into what went wrong. When it was over, Crosbie gathered the Sto:lo chiefs in a Vancouver hotel room and apologized with all the grace and eloquence a Newfoundlander can muster. "Mistakes were made," he conceded, "but they were mistakes of the heart."

Pearse's findings were doomed. Most fishermen had decided they weren't going to believe anything he had to say. For one thing, Pearse had already declared his aversion to the "inefficient", ragtag coastal small-boat fleet in his royal commission inquiry into the fishing industry ten years earlier. In his royal commission findings, Pearse had recognized the eventual reality of revitalized tribal fisheries but counselled against the continuation of all those troublesome little gillnetters and trollers when technology provided such cost-effective alternatives. "Ultimately, they might not need any boats at all," he once said. And it didn't help much that he was on the board of directors of the Aluminum Company of Canada, which had wrecked the salmon-rich Nechako River with its Kemano hydroelectric project. Alcan's operations had produced low water levels and high water temperatures in the upper Fraser that had contributed to major fish kills, but Pearse didn't consider those impacts particularly significant in 1992. He took ten weeks and a $48,000 cheque to conclude that the Department of Fisheries and Oceans' estimate of the numbers of fish Natives caught was short by about 200,000 sockeye.

Larkin's efforts, described as a mere "technical appendix" to Pearse's report, painted a much more illuminating picture. Larkin found that if there were sockeye that went missing upstream of Mission Bridge in 1992 at all, it certainly wasn't the first time. The numbers hadn't been adding up for at least a decade. "Whatever had been responsible for the phenomenon of

missing fish seemed to have been in effect for a few years preceding 1992," Larkin maintained. But 1992 was different, Larkin
said, and it wasn't just because some Indian bands were selling
their fish openly. Larkin pointed out that water levels in the
Fraser were so low in 1992, they were breaking all known
records, and the water was warmer in the river than it had been
in at least sixteen years. Dead fish had been floating downriver
all summer. Larkin didn't dismiss Alcan's role in fish kills, either.
"Since the Kenney dam was constructed [on the Nechako] ...
there were significant mortalities of Early Stuart [sockeye] in
association with high temperatures and low discharge," he
found. In 1992, high temperatures and low water levels caused
"significant mortality" of Fraser River salmon.

Larkin looked at all the possible factors – errors in the count of
sockeye passing Mission Bridge, the numbers of fish the Indians
caught, the numbers that could be attributed to "poaching", the
numbers of fish that died from natural causes, and the estimates
of spawners. He concluded that if the estimates in only two of
those variables were off by a few percent, "then all the remainder
is more than accounted for". Larkin said his "best-guess scenario" was that a number of variables were slightly off. Once
high temperatures and other factors were taken into account,
"all the fish are accounted for."

There was no "biological disaster" on the Fraser River in
1992. It's true that fewer spawners made it than DFO's preseason
plans had called for. Unfortunately, that's a routine occurrence
in DFO fisheries management. But when all was said and done,
the number of sockeye that reached their Fraser River spawning
grounds in 1992 had been exceeded only once on that cycle year
in half a century. If there was anyone to thank for that, it was the
Petrunia brothers, Wayne Crawford, Vince and Barry Manuck,

and the hundreds of Fraser River gillnetters who were shut out of the river in 1992, along with hundreds of Sto:lo fishermen whose nets were pulled from the river after having caught 100,000 fewer fish than their preseason agreements allowed.

In spite of those sacrifices, the commercial catch of Fraser River sockeye in 1992 was still the highest it had been on that cycle year since the 1940s. The beneficiaries were the companies that make up the coastal monopoly and the seiners that reaped the bonanza in Juan de Fuca Strait on both sides of the border. None of these facts, however, got in the way of the story that B.C.'s mass media continued to present to a public that was already nervous and confused about aboriginal rights and land claims. The story was often based on nothing more substantial than a news release from the B.C. Fisheries Survival Coalition, which had become the main rallying point for anti-Native hostilities since it was founded in January, 1993 with contributions from a wide field of concerns, including the B.C. Cattlemen's Association. Stories referring to 1992's "poaching" and "missing fish" continued on an almost daily basis for months into 1993 and beyond. Journalists continued to report "news" based on the assumption that tribal fisheries were taking a bigger share of the catch. There was no tribal-share increase in 1992. Federal bureaucrats were insisting that any increases after 1992 should be kept to less than two percent of the coast-wide total allowable catch of salmon to match a reduction in fishing boats (a longtime demand of the Fisheries Council) through a licence-retirement scheme funded with public money. Typical of the coverage was a January 1993 *Province* newspaper editorial under the headline "The Way of All Fish", which asserted: "Since the native fishery was expanded following court decisions enforced by Ottawa, the salmon available to commercial fishermen have dwindled alarmingly." In fact, the opposite was true, on both counts. Fisheries Council president Mike Hunter continued to go unchallenged in his claims that the Aboriginal Fisheries Strategy "is destroying the economy of British Columbia". And when seiner Bob Rezansoff, spokesman for the B.C. Fisheries Survival Coalition said "people up and down the coast are not going to [sit by and] see their entire livelihoods disappear", never was there any evidence presented of a single commercial fisherman who had lost his livelihood to the Sparrow decision or the Aboriginal Fisheries Strategy.

Some newspapers scoured the landscape for evidence of rapacious Indians and wanton excess. The *Chilliwack Progress* of December 3, 1992, placed on its front page an article with the headline: "Native Fishery Raises Health Concerns in Yale – Lack of Control Led to a Mess in the Streets". The story documents the complaints of the Fraser Cheam Regional District about Indians peeing in the bushes during the fishing season. This came from a regional district that every day was dumping thousands of gallons of untreated sewage directly into the Fraser River. By February 1993, the hostilities enflamed by all the disinformation associated with the Aboriginal Fisheries Strategy had spread to the classrooms in coastal towns like Campbell River, where aboriginal and non-aboriginal children were reported to be fighting amongst themselves. And it's no wonder, with advertisements like this appearing in the local newspapers: "The wholesale slaughter of salmon and wildlife in B.C. must be stopped now; Your children have a right to hunt and fish ... no one has the right to extort others for the right to fish and hunt in B.C." The advertisement went on to promote a February 27 Fisheries Survival Coalition rally at the legislature in Victoria. About 2,500 protesters turned up. They carried placards that read "Fraser River salmon – RIP 1992" and the like. Scores of the protesters weren't even fishermen. They came from as far away as Prince George.

By April, when fishermen's union secretary-treasurer Dennis
Brown explained to fishermen in Maple Ridge that "the industry
is up for grabs [and] we have no other choice but to retaliate,"
the hysteria had actually spread to Interior municipalities that
had no known association with any segment of the fishing industry. One of the first to take the bait was the Municipality of Summerland. Municipal council decided to protest against the
Aboriginal Fisheries Strategy on the argument that if they didn't,
Natives would soon be using the Sparrow decision to gain access
to unrestricted quantities of timber – by pursuing a "ceremonial"
right to totem poles. The April 19 edition of the *Penticton Her-
ald* reported Summerland's decision by describing the federal
government's policy as one that "allows natives to catch and sell
unrestricted amounts of salmon without proper licencing or regulatory or enforcement control."

And as the salmon were spending their final days in saltwater,
making their way back to the Fraser River in June of 1993, B.C.'s
newspapers were carrying fishing-industry advertisements with
the same old graphs and pie charts showing the high percentage
of Natives already employed in the fishing industry. There were
pictures of happy Indian cannery workers. There were more
brave words at the dock about what should be done about the
"bad" Indians who weren't willing to leave well enough alone.
White fishermen throughout the coast were talking about taking
matters into their own hands. More "Oka in reverse" talk. In a
June 1 letter to its members, the Fisheries Survival Coalition
boasted: "If not for the coalition, almost every Aboriginal band
with access to salmon and herring would be allowed to sell it this
year." It was an unusual claim, since only three of more than
eighty Aboriginal Fisheries Strategy agreements (lower Fraser,
Nuu-Chah-Nulth, and Skeena) made mention of fish sales, and a
succession of fisheries ministers have been telling everybody since

the summer of 1992 that it was going to stay that way. Meanwhile, the union's Dennis Brown – a key spokesman for the
coalition – was telling the *Vancouver Sun* that if there was violence between Indians and whites fishing in the Fraser River, it
would not be his fault, it would be the government's fault, and he
would hold the federal government "solely accountable". He
assured the newspaper that he, personally, would do his best to
prevent his members from attacking Indians. In its June 5 article
reporting Brown's comments, the *Sun* reported: "Last year, the
native fishery was blamed after an alleged 1.2 million sockeye
counted at Mission Bridge failed to arrive at the spawning
grounds further upstream. White fishers blamed natives for the
loss." Never mind the fact that nothing of the kind actually happened. The sky was falling. The Indians were to blame.

I never did go back to the *Vancouver Sun*. I moved away
from Annacis Channel in 1993. It wasn't easy watching Queensborough get buried under subdivisions, and if B.C. was going to
become enflamed by the same degree of racial animosity and hysteria that swept the coast in 1992 – a phenomenon I had certainly never witnessed in such intensity in the more than fifteen
years that I had worked as a journalist in this province – I'd
decided it was best to ride it out somewhere else. After everything had been packed into the moving trucks, I took one last
look around.

From the roof of my houseboat, I could still see the ridge
above Saint Mungo's on the far side of the river, across the roofs
of the new complex of warehouses that had gone up beside the
sewage-treatment plant on Annacis Island. I was just a boy when
I was first drawn by the wooded ravines that cut deep into that
ridge, when it had seemed to hover in the morning clouds above

the great expanse of the delta and the bog. But now the Alex Fraser Bridge towered above the ridge, carrying tens of thousands of commuters from new subdivisions to their jobs in Vancouver, and the bridge abutments dug into the detritus of a fishing village the Musqueam called Suwq'eqsun'. It's one of the oldest known sites of human settlement in Canada. For as long as eight thousand years, the people there harvested salmon and oolichan and sturgeon from piers suspended from pilings jutting into the river, and they lived in cavernous plank houses in those ravines. After the smallpox, the white fishermen who built their houses there, on the hills above the Saint Mungo's and Glenrose canneries, used to say that there were so many bones they were sticking out of the ground, and when the winds were strong they would fall from burial boxes in the trees.

In their turn, all that was left of the canneries were the burned-out stubs of pilings sticking out of the mud. The great Fraser River salmon runs declined, and control of B.C. salmon fell into fewer and fewer hands until by 1993 only two salmon canneries remained on the Fraser: an Ocean Fisheries canning line up by Deas dock and a small non-union line in Ladner. The Premier Cannery, Cleeve, Westminster, Wadham's, Harlock, and Wellington, all of them gone, their pilings sticking up between the weeds like the ribs of the Japanese gillnet boats that poked through the mud over by the old Annieville Dyke, where they had been rafted together after they were confiscated in 1942 and left to break up in the storms that spring. And somewhere in one of those ravines were the remains of an old China House, one of the dreary barns where Chinese cannery hands were housed before the invention of a mechanical gang knife eliminated them from the industry. The canning companies called the machine the "Iron Chink".

Upriver, the *Joy-Ethel*, the *Slo-Poke*, the *Panther*, the *Escorial*, the *Three Sons*, and all the other gillnetters swayed at their moorings. The view of the river that cold spring morning didn't leave all that much hope for their future.

Still, the descendants of Suwq'eqsun' survived somehow. Although they are diminished, they live on at Musqueam and Katzie and Coquitlam and Tsawwassen. Maybe there's a lesson in this somewhere, I thought, for all of us.

The salmon had survived all this, too, if only in remnants. They'll always take a mile when they're only allowed an inch, and they can rebound from the hardest assaults. They had survived 1913, when the railroad companies blasted the side of a mountain into the Fraser River at Hell's Gate. They survived the onslaught of the canneries. They had survived just about everything we had thrown at them, and on that last morning in Annacis Channel, in February 1993, the salmon that were heading towards the Fraser River were massing in greater numbers than anything we'd seen in a long, long time. More than seventeen million sockeye salmon. More than thirty million pink salmon.

Out there in the big rolling pasture of the Pacific Ocean, salmon survival rates depend on the amount of feed, the temperature of the ocean, the success of predators that rely on salmon, and a host of other factors. For the salmon returning in 1993, the pastures of the sea had been kind, and survival rates were high. In 1994, survival rates were low. To make matters worse, it was fish-war time again. Canada and the United States couldn't agree on how many fish each country should intercept. The Pacific Salmon Commission first reckoned there were ten million sockeye coming home in 1994, then they weren't so sure. The Fisheries Council of B.C. made its contribution to resolving the dilemma by sending Mike Hunter to a meeting of the Canadian members of the Pacific Salmon Commission to remind them that there was a fish war on and it might just be necessary to "sacrifice a few fish". In the end, the sockeye barely limped home to their spawning beds in 1994. In the case of the Adams River sockeye, only about 700,000 made it home – about two million fewer than planned. In total, after the Canadian commercial fleet took more than nine million sockeye and American boats took two million more, fewer than three million Fraser sockeye spawned that year. Still, all summer long, B.C.'s daily newspapers and television news shows were full of reports about Indian poaching. To make its case, a BCTV series on the subject dredged up five-year-old accounts of a "sting" operation in the Fraser Valley and a four-year-old story about an enforcement action in Port Alberni, and after several weeks of effort, with Fisheries Survival Coalition members mobilized to come up with evidence for the cameras, BCTV's total amassed evidence of fish caught illegally by Indians amounted to five salmon.

In 1995, it was the same story all over again. The sockeye had not survived their ocean sojourn in healthy numbers, and times were so tough that some gillnetters never made it to fishing openings because they couldn't afford the fuel. For the third year in a row, the industry worked overtime to convince everybody that the Indians were the problem. The federal government's response was to take about half the fish allocated to the Sto:lo in 1995's agreements and reallocate the fish to the commercial fleet. Upriver from the Sto:lo, the entire Native catch amounted to about four fish per person to fulfil the food, social, and ceremonial needs of about 20,000 Native people for the entire year. On the coast, the situation was worse. Ottawa promised the Pacheenaht an opportunity to harvest 3,500 sockeye. Their catch: zero. The Ditidaht were promised 3,000 sockeye. Their catch was zero. The Cowichan tribes were promised 20,000. Their catch was 2,000.

And on it went while the commercial fishery continued in Juan de Fuca and Johnstone straits, despite the admonition of the Supreme Court judges in the 1990 Sparrow decision: "If, in a given year, conservation needs required a reduction in the number of fish such that the number equalled the number required for food for the Indians, then all the fish available after conservation would go to the Indians according to the constitutional nature of their fishing right." So much for the Constitution.

Still, more and more, my Queensborough neighbours, along with small-boat fishermen everywhere on the coast, were proving smarter than the leaders of their union. They were rejecting all the entreaties and anti-Indian rallying cries of the industry lobbyists. More and more, they were finding ways to work with their upriver neighbours in the Native fisheries. As late as July 1996, opinion leaders like CKNW radio hotline host Rafe Mair were still blaming the Aboriginal Fisheries Strategy and Indian poaching for the calamities that had befallen the Fraser's sockeye runs. Because of poor ocean survival rates that affected the 1994 and 1995 sockeye runs, federal fisheries scientists were hedging their bets and no commercial openings were initially planned on the four-year-old fish returning in 1996. Mair took this to prove that the industry was "reaping the whirlwind" of the aboriginal fisheries of 1992. All the smart people from the Fisheries Survival Coalition said the 1992 runs were so battered by Indian poachers that it would be decades, if ever again, that the 1992 cycle year would be strong enough to support another fishery. But in 1996, as July turned to August, the offspring of the 1992 sockeye started showing up off Sand Heads at the mouth of the Fraser. They kept coming and coming and coming, in numbers so great even the best federal scientists were confused by it all, and 1996 proved to be the third-largest sockeye return to the Fraser on that cycle year since 1912. All those fishermen that believed the Coalition's predictions had chosen to fish the North Coast or applied to have their licence renewals suspended for the season. Those that kept their heads fished the Fraser in 1996. It was a great year. It was not a miracle.

This is not about miracles.

What this all comes down to is survival and the fact that there are still ancient cycles at work out there. There are forces that shape the way we live, and we flourish or we die by how well we understand them, or at least by how well we recognize they exist, or by how well we try to make some coherent sense of them, and by how well we adapt to those things we may never really understand all that well. Much has been made of the miracle of Pacific salmon, the way they arise from gravel beds in glacier-fed streams splashing down from the Rockies, the way they tumble downstream to the sea and swim so far they come within sight of the mountains of Kamchatka, and the way they find the route back home, somehow. But this is not about miracles. This is about survival.

If there is a miracle in this, it is that after everything we have done to them, they come home to us at all.

Spirit
Dancers

Liumchen Canyon is a morning's walk upstream
from the place where the Chilliwack River tumbles through a
mountain corridor into the Fraser Valley, about a hundred kilometres east of Vancouver. Liumchen is one of several canyons
that rise southward into the mountains above the Chilliwack
River. The spirit dancers used to come here. They came in the
autumn months, at sunrise, to swim in the stone-walled pools
beneath the cliff edge where Larry Commodore and I were sitting, in a grove of maple and willow. Below, in the gorge, someone had spray-painted the word PUSSY on a strange green
boulder cradled in a crevice above a small cave. All along the

creek, campsites were cut into the trees. The debris of McDonald's restaurants and 7-Elevens littered the ground.

"You can see why the dancers don't come here anymore," Commodore said.

It had been almost ten years since that morning when Commodore looked out his front-room window and saw a group of spirit dancers arriving in their cars and pickup trucks. They were across a field from his house at Soowahlie, a reserve community of about two hundred people hidden in the hills above the bridge at Vedder Crossing. The dancers were dressed in their leggings and shawls. They were carrying their life poles. They wandered off into the bush to bathe in a nearby creek. The same scene repeated itself several times in the following days. "I figured it was pretty strange," Commodore said. "Why would they pick this place, so close, on the reserve?" Commodore went next door, where his mother lives, to ask her about what he was seeing. She'd been initiated into the spirit-dance society years earlier. One question led to another, and he talked to other people about it, and what Commodore soon learned was that the younger dancers from throughout the Sto:lo territory, stretching from Langley to Spuzzum, were finding that the old places, their "training grounds", were disappearing.

On Chilliwack Mountain and Sumas Mountain, two ancient landmarks on the south bank of the Fraser River, sacred pools and similar sites were becoming lost to subdivisions with names like Maple Hills Classic Country Townhomes. The young dancers would find themselves stumbling out of the trees onto cul-de-sacs with names like Huckleberry Place and Sunrise Drive.

Larry Commodore was not a spirit dancer. He was a band councillor at Soowahlie and he held the environment portfolio for the Sto:lo Tribal Council. He kept to his own spiritual practices, and although he respected the spirit dance, it just wasn't for him. It's a lifelong commitment that demands rigorous discipline from its adherents.

The dancers follow a harsh and complex way of life that is guarded by a tradition of secrecy, and many dancers spend several weeks of the year preoccupied with the winter ceremonial season, travelling to longhouses throughout the Coast Salish area, from Vancouver Island to Washington state. The spirit dance underwent a tremendous revival after laws banning such practices were struck from the Indian Act in 1951. Back then, there were less than a dozen dancers left in the Sto:lo territory, which takes in the entire Fraser Valley. By the 1990s, there were more than seven hundred, from Pitt Meadows to Yale. As for the Sto:lo's huge winter ceremonial houses, there were none left in 1951. By 1995, there were six.

Frank Malloway carries the name Siyemchess. The name has been handed down through his family, and it came from one of four brothers who played pivotal roles in the history of the old Chilliwack tribe. The brothers lived at the old "Watery Eaves Longhouse" village in the Chilliwack River Valley. The village has long since been eroded away into the river, partly due to logging. Anthropologists put the time of Siyemchess and his brothers at about AD 1400. Malloway was initiated in the late 1970s, and before he was sixty years old, he was considered one of the older dancers after having spent fifteen winters in the longhouse – or smokehouse, as many Sto:lo call the central institution of the spirit dance. It had been years since Malloway built his own longhouse at Yakweakwioose, and he had helped bring scores of new dancers into the tradition, but by the early 1990s he had come to worry that the younger dancers' syowen – their spirit power – would not prove as strong as the old days because the young dancers didn't have the same powerful places where they could train. A growing number of dancers from throughout the Sto:lo territory were turning to the more remote corners of the Chilliwack River Valley for their training grounds at the same time that the valley was being broken wide open to the outside world. "And thirty years from now," Malloway asked one day when we were talking about the situation, "where are the dancers going to go then?"

The sun was falling behind Liumchen Mountain. In the willows, Larry Commodore sat quietly. He wore a blue T-shirt, blue jeans, and his black hair was pulled back in a ponytail. He was forty, and he didn't look like he fit the reputation he had developed for himself over the years. When he was young, he was in and out of school and in and out of his home, which was the scene of the kind of alcoholism and violence so often associated with the poverty of reserves. He spent part of his youth in a white foster home in Yarrow, where he remembers his foster parents as "nice white folks, but not my folks", and he spent part of his early adulthood in jail, where his first sentence, five months, was for breaking and entering. He broke into a secondhand store in downtown Chilliwack to steal a typewriter. It was because he wanted to try coming to terms with what he saw happening around him by writing poetry instead of punching out cops. But that was then. Larry Commodore ended up becoming what he modestly called a "grassroots organizer". It had become his life-long commitment, as it had for an emerging generation of like-minded First Nations activists. Commodore was there during the Fred Quilt hearings in the early 1970s. He was there at Oka in 1990. He chose not to place much faith in band-council politics or tribal-council politics. Not that he didn't respect the chiefs and tribal leaders. It was just that, like the spirit dance, their approach was not for him.

While Commodore was learning what the spirit dancers were up against, and why Liumchen Canyon was lost to them, he was also finding out that all the other side valleys above the Chilliwack River were facing a similar fate. Westward from Chilliwack Lake there is the Centre Creek valley, Nesakwatch Creek, Slesse Creek, Tamihi Creek, and, finally, Liumchen. All these valleys had been "training grounds" for the spirit dancers. What wasn't logged already was set to be logged. Where there wasn't logging, there were campsites, recreational vehicles, and mountain bikes. Commodore reckoned that something had to be done. He decided to try and help organize the spirit dancers in defence of their sacred places. In the spring of 1988, Commodore started travelling around the Fraser Valley, talking to spirit dancers, talking to leading elders in the longhouse, trying to develop some means to keep sacred places safe for those practices that are so central to the spirit-dance tradition.

"I figured that we had to do something. We had to get together and get organized, pretty soon, before it was too late," Commodore said, his voice rising just enough to be heard over the roar of the stream below us. "But it seemed like everything was working against me."

What Commodore found himself up against was the same complex phenomenon that had kept the spirit dance hidden behind a solid cultural wall since white settlement began to transform the Sto:lo territories in the 1800s. Silence and secrecy had always been an effective defence. What the white people don't know, they're less likely to wreck, the argument went. Why change it? "There's a feeling that it's best not to say anything,"

Commodore said. "They figure people will ridicule them. They'll say they're making it up. That's what's behind the reluctance of a lot of the spiritual people to be openly fighting for and defending their space. Who would want to open up their spirituality to ridicule?"

Earlier in the day, we had walked along a ridge near Liumchen Peak. If the Fraser Valley had a roof, this place would be on the edge of it. We could see from a point near Rosedale in the east to the encroaching subdivisions of Clearbrook in the west. The ridge was surrounded by clearcuts that scarred the mountainsides all along the north and south walls of the Chilliwack River Valley. On our way up, we had come across a small grove of old growth, left over from the early days of logging when patches were left as firebreaks. Among the trees in one of the few groves of old growth left on the mountainside were several cedars from which bark had been stripped many years before for baskets, or capes, or hats. Archaeologists call them culturally modified trees. Throughout the Chilliwack River Valley, even the old firebreaks were falling to forest companies as good timber became more scarce and cutblocks moved deeper and higher into the mountains. In the valley below us, the extent of urban encroachment into the Sto:lo heartland was vivid, despite the layer of smog that meteorologists were comparing to the blanket of pollution that routinely covers Los Angeles. Below us lay the sprawling District of Chilliwack, only an hour or so east of Vancouver on the Trans-Canada Highway. Chilliwack had been booming with the construction of commuter-pod neighbourhoods – streets without sidewalks and houses that mimic the beige, vinyl-sided monster-home style of Surrey and Delta. Chilliwack's population had grown from 40,000 in 1984 to 60,000 in 1994. It was expected to reach 100,000 by 2004. The neighbouring municipalities of

Abbotsford, Matsqui, and Sumas were growing just as fast. Inundated by the arrival of the suburbs were the Sto:lo communities of Popkum, Cheam, Kwakwawapilt, Aitchelitz, Squiala, Skwah, Skway, Yakweakwioose, Skowkale, Tzeachten, and Soowahlie. The people in these small reserve communities numbered about 3,000.

While the suburbs were growing, Sto:lo Tribal Council anthropologist Gordon Mohs was working against time, trying to document the extent of the loss of Sto:lo sacred sites. In an extensive study, Mohs found that suburban encroachment, intensified logging activity, and increased recreational activities had accelerated a cycle of destruction that began in the 1800s. Of two hundred Sto:lo sacred sites examined, "50 sites have been destroyed, 50 damaged or disturbed. Another 25 face ongoing disturbance or potential destruction from development." There are more than fifty recorded village sites in the central valley area, so it was difficult to put a shovel in the ground anywhere without the risk of disturbing some archaeological evidence of the extent of Sto:lo settlement. Before smallpox and other diseases so drastically diminished their population, Mohs reckons there might have been up to 30,000 Sto:lo people who lived in towns and villages along the Fraser below Spuzzum. When Simon Fraser passed through in 1808, he encountered a house, in the vicinity of what is now Sumas, more than two football fields in length: "The whole range, which is 640 feet long by 60 broad, is under one roof. The front is 18 feet high, and the cover is slanting. All the apartments, which are separated in portions, are square, excepting the Chief's, which is 90 feet long."

The loss of archaeological sites was one thing. But the loss of sacred sites, and sites of ethnic, historical, or ceremonial significance to the Sto:lo, was greater. Sacred sites were afforded no protection under B.C.'s heritage-conservation laws. A place where some graduate student had unearthed a seventeenth-century fire pit might qualify for some nominal protection, but a place inhabited by water beings who have maintained a relationship with a particular Sto:lo community since the beginning of time did not. Although the Heritage Conservation Act provided penalties for wilfully robbing or destroying registered archaeological sites, sites of profound historical or spiritual significance to First Nations in British Columbia remained outside legislative protection. Of the nineteen thousand heritage sites listed on the B.C. government's provincewide registry by the 1990s (a heritage site is defined as a site of "historic, architectural, archeological, paleontological or scenic significance"), only a half dozen were recorded under a general "Ceremonial/Myth" classification.

Despite his efforts, what confounded Mohs was the vast cultural gulf that has always influenced relations between Native and non-Native people in British Columbia. It was not easy incorporating Sto:lo values in regional planning when these values could only be accurately described within their own conceptual framework and in the Halq'emeylem language. Stl'itl'aqem is "a spirited place". Sxwoxwiyam is a place associated with an important ancestral event. The B.C. government was trying to come to grips with the problem. A series of amendments to the Heritage Conservation Act were adopted by the legislature, including increased penalties for destroying heritage sites – from fines of $2,000 and six months' jail time to fines of $1 million and two years' jail time. The heritage branch was also in the process of developing a first-ever, comprehensive, provincewide heritage-resource inventory. Patrick Frey, the Heritage Branch's assistant director, said the inventory would provide the first real opportunity to ensure that sacred sites were afforded heritage-site protection. He said the great hope was that B.C. might conclude agreements with various First Nations that would establish inventories of such sites: "That's a very significant provision, but it will take time to implement, and only time will tell if it will work."

In the Chilliwack area, there were places where spirit beings were still seen. There was also Minter Gardens. There were places where the Thunderbird lived. There was also Flintstones Bedrock City. There were creeks long associated with the seelke, the legendary two-headed serpent. There were centuries-old sun-ceremony sites and important places for first-salmon ceremonies and offerings to the dead. There were also two water slides, the Rainbow Country Inn, the Hemlock Valley ski resort, and Harrison Hot Springs (a sacred site lost long ago). There were buried villages, haunted places, medicinal springs, red-ochre quarries, and strange-looking rocks that are believed to be Sto:lo ancestors who were turned to stone. There was also a sign on the freeway: "Chilliwack – Open for Business: Call the Mayor – 792-9311".

Cultus Lake takes its name from the old Chinook-jargon word for "worthless". Although that fact might be known to many Fraser Valley residents, few know why such a beautiful lake is described that way. The name derives from an old story that ends in a tragic death, and it involves the evil doings of a sorcerer whose body was pushed into the lake. "Two Doctors' Rock" was a site central to the saga. A house was built on top of it. A maple grove enclosing an ancient burial ground near Yakweak-wioose village just outside Sardis was excluded from the Yak-weakwioose reserve early in this century and the trees were cut down. At least fifty such burial sites in the area have been destroyed or disturbed.

X:als is the most important figure in Sto:lo spiritual traditions. The old people sometimes refer to X:als as "the little Christ", because it was X:als who travelled throughout the known world, separating people from animals and generally bringing order to society. Among the most prominent marks X:als left on the landscape are "stone people", known also as transformer sites. Usually, they are the remains of selfish people or despotic leaders X:als punished by turning them to stone, to stand as cautionary reminders for the generations to come. One such stone person was Kwiyaxtel, a shaman X:als transformed near Yale. The Kwiyaxtel stone was destroyed during the construction of a tunnel early in the 1900s. Another shaman X:als turned to stone was destroyed during the construction of a private road along Hope Slough in Chilliwack. By the 1990s, fourteen such sites had been destroyed.

Sometimes, these sites are lost because Sto:lo people years ago deliberately hid them. Old Sto:lo people still tell stories about several pictograph and petroglyph sites in the Fraser Canyon area that were buried around the turn of the century for fear that white people would destroy them. And sometimes, sacramental objects are disturbed by well-meaning non-Natives. Cedar life poles and the regalia of spirit-dance initiates are traditionally hidden away deep in the forest, often tied to saplings, to symbolically rejoin the life of the trees from which they came. The sites are generally known only to the dancer. A well-intentioned logger showed up at the provincial Forests Ministry's district offices in Agassiz with a life pole he found, hoping to return it to its rightful owner. A few months earlier, a hunter showed up with a life pole at the Chilliwack Museum. He found it in the mountains above the Chilliwack River Valley.

Mohs had been conducting archaeological studies in the Sto:lo territories for twenty years, and he said it had taken all that time for Sto:lo elders to decide to speak openly about the importance of spiritual sites. "It's a big problem," he said. "Native heritage concerns are not taken into account in municipal and regional development planning. A lot of the older people say we should start talking about these things now. But there are still a lot of Sto:lo people who think these things should be kept quiet."

The old tactic of silence was becoming more difficult to maintain. As suburban development encroached upon Sto:lo villages, ancient dusk-to-dawn winter ceremonials that attracted several hundred people at a time were taking place under the very noses of tens of thousands of commuters who had fled the city for more affordable building lots in the Fraser Valley. Rarely was any public light shed on the ancient traditions taking place in their midst. To most Fraser Valley residents, the great ceremonial longhouses on the Sto:lo reserves were probably just oversized barns. Sometimes, a flurry of controversy would erupt when a spirit dancer died somewhere in the Coast Salish area during the rigorous initiation rites (about a dozen initiates died between 1960 and 1990), or the winter-long ceremonies would prompt letters to the *Chilliwack Progress* from recently arrived subdivision residents complaining of sleepless nights and demanding some sort of bylaw restraint against the incessant drum pounding from the nearby reserve. Beyond that, the non-Native public remained unaware that although they were living in what was advertised as an adult single-family community only minutes from the Cottonwood Mall, they also lived in a country that was shaped by the hand of X:als, the Transformer, and the very mountains around them were once people whose fate had been recounted in stories told and retold down through the generations, in this very valley, for thousands of years.

Wayne Kelly was a new dancer in 1994. He was twenty-nine, and it was his fourth winter "in the smokehouse". Like many spirit dancers I've talked with about these questions, Kelly offered encouragement and help, but he also asked that not much of what was said end up written down. But Kelly would say this: "I'm just a baby. I've only been in a little while, and there's so much I'm still learning, but if you write things down on paper, it can belong to anybody. Who knows what will happen. But still, if the population keeps coming in and these places aren't there anymore, where are we going to go?"

Larry Commodore didn't pretend to have all the answers. All he reckoned was that grassroots organizing, alliance-building, and cooperative political action beat the alternatives. That was the point he wanted to make sure I understood as we left Liumchen Canyon, as the sun was falling behind the mountains. He said he figured that if nothing else, maybe he could at least make a difference up there, in the Chilliwack River Valley. This was the traditional territory of the Soowahlie and the heartland of the Chilliwack tribe, one of the dozen or so divisions of the old Sto:lo nation. The Chilliwack River Valley was one of the last redoubts of the spirit dancers and one of the few sparsely populated regions left in the Lower Mainland. Everybody wanted a piece of it, and the stakes were getting higher with the passing days. The "Fraser Coalition for Sustainable Forests" – the forest industry's local public front – wanted the status quo, and they had pulled out all the stops in a typical anti-environmentalist crusade. The last thing Commodore wanted was the status quo. He wanted horse logging for the unemployed workers on his reserve. He had already put the Coalition on notice that they were going to have to deal with the Soowahlie people.

The Western Canada Wilderness Committee wanted the Chilliwack Valley set aside as a protected area, linking it up with a proposal that would scale down industrial forestry over a massive swath of the entire North Cascades on both sides of the Canada-U.S. border. One day in 1993, the WCWC's Joe Foy remembers, "This guy named Larry Commodore walks into my office in Vancouver and demands to know who I think I am, talking about what should happen to his land." Commodore and Foy soon became friends. Foy said he would only want a park if it were established in cooperation with the tribal interests in the valley, but he readily admitted that even cut-and-run forest practices may actually do less damage to the spirit dancers' interests than a badly planned park that produces year-round flotillas of motor homes.

The District of Chilliwack had plans of its own for the Chilliwack River Valley area. The district's growth projections anticipated that the population of Promontory Mountain – the site of another ancient village – would grow from 330 to 5,000 in ten years, and that on nearby Ryder Mountain, another development would see population grow from 1,000 to 9,000 in ten years. The Chilliwack River Valley Ratepayers Association, meanwhile, wanted things left alone.

"I don't have any grand strategy about how it's going to pull together," Commodore said. "And it's not like I've got some plan to reclaim the land or anything. It's really a matter of the land reclaiming me. And I'm reaching out to those people who respect the land, and who want to respect it and protect it. It's like being up in the mountains. Sometimes, you can't see much more than what's around you. You can't see over into the next valley. You just do what you have to do, where you are, to survive."

Our Way or the Highway

It is January 20, 1995, at the downtown Vancouver offices of the Council of Forest Industries, the lobby group for B.C.'s big forest firms. In the boardroom, the members of COFI's committee on aboriginal affairs are wrestling with a difficult question. One of the executives is taking minutes.

The COFI committee has been advised that the Nisga'a leadership, which formed its first land-claims committee in 1890, was reluctantly considering a government "offer" that would total $60,000 for each of the 6,000 members of the tribe, 200,000 hectares of land, and fishing-rights guarantees. It was one of several scenarios that federal, provincial, and Nisga'a negotiators had been trading back and forth. It amounted to about one-tenth of the original Nisga'a position.

The COFI executives discuss Native logging-company failures in Alaska and clearcut logging on Alberta reserves, and there is a comment that if B.C. Natives regain some control over the fisheries resource, they will "liquidate it". And there is this: "I suppose there is no need for Natives to worry about tomorrow, the government will always look after them. They see it as today's lifestyle being better than yesterday's. Proof that the white people owe them something."

The minutes describe the dilemma at hand. Nisga'a settlement lands "cannot be expropriated" once a treaty is signed. Should COFI "continue to argue that the governments are giving too much away" or simply "push" the Nisga'a to accept the deal, then fight it out in public in the hopes the government would back away from it?

Whoever it was that recorded the session, Marly Beets, COFI's vice-president of aboriginal affairs, insisted that it wasn't her. She said they weren't the secretary's minutes, either. She said her COFI colleagues were furious about the document's disclosure, but she wasn't about to conduct a "witch-hunt" to find out who it was, and the minutes didn't accurately reflect what happened at the meeting anyway. It's just that there was a lot of "militant" talk on both sides, Beets said, and besides, people talked that way about the forest industry all the time. She said COFI would like nothing better than cooperation between Native communities and forest firms, and COFI had no objection to forestry components in treaties as long as governments could find companies willing to sell forest tenures to allow such arrangements.

The meeting minutes do not show what strategy COFI opted

to pursue against the government "offer" to the Nisga'a. But two weeks later, the "offer" had been leaked to the *Globe and Mail*. The backlash was overwhelming. There was talk of violence and secret government giveaways. The "offer" was gone, and the Nisga'a talks were badly damaged.

The minutes state that the next item on the January 20 agenda was a delegation from the federal Reform party's aboriginal task force, consisting of Reform party adviser Brice MacDougall, Edith McKay (Skeena MP Mike Scott's aboriginal-affairs assistant), and Bob Head, task-force "leader". Head was an RCMP negotiator during the Oka crisis.

There is no reason to regard such a person as in any way an unusual participant in these sorts of discussions. For more than two years, it had been as though British Columbia was under some sort of siege.

Crack Down on Native Lawbreakers, the headlines said. Government-Sponsored Blackmail. How the Northwest Was Lost. Land Given by God and the NDP to the Okanagan Forever. Natives Claim 110 Per Cent of Province. Secret Pact With Haida. Secret Dealing With Natives. Public Silenced on Land Claims. Inter-Tribal War Flows From Nass River Overlap. Private Land Now Subject To Rights. Land Claims Secrecy.

In the bedlam following disclosure of the tentative Nisga'a deal, Skeena Reform MP Mike Scott warned that if negotiators concluded the kind of treaty that was on the table, there would be "social unrest like never seen before. ... Yes, by non-Native people. We are so close to violence in rural B.C. that it's not funny."

While the Nisga'a treaty panic was still in full swing, Scott signed a letter and sent it to Ottawa's *Hill Times*, attacking proposed federal gun-control laws on the grounds that only an "armed citizenry" could defend itself against "those who seek unlimited power for government". When his remarks caused trouble for party leader Preston Manning, Scott tried to tidy up the situation by saying a staff member had actually written the letter. But Scott later told Sterling news service he had several reasons to suspect a dictatorship could be in store for Canada, and "it certainly makes the government a lot more comfortable when they feel the citizens are unarmed."

A year earlier, during some other alarm he set off about the Nisga'a talks, Scott said: "If we think we've seen problems at Oka or other parts of Canada with confrontation, we haven't seen anything yet. I'm not a scaremonger, but I hear it every day. It's frightening."

It was an easy plot to follow.

They are not like us. They do not have to work or pay taxes. Deep within our own government, their sympathizers are busy implementing a secret agenda to carve up our province into warring mini-states. We have already lost most of the North. They are creating a new order, with special rights enjoyed by a small racial minority. Unless they're stopped, they will enshrine this regime in the Constitution. Forever.

It is hysteria. It was not a new phenomenon in British Columbia. By 1995, land-claims hysteria had moved from the domain of eccentrics on the outskirts of towns like Smithers, Ucluelet, and Blue River to the centre of B.C.'s land-use debates.

Hysteria has tended to insinuate itself into B.C.'s mainstream when the economy is unstable and the future is obscured behind dark clouds. The world becomes too complicated for the news media to explain, the best-financed conspiracy theory gets a free ride downtown, civil discourse degenerates into paranoia, and the next thing you know, it's nightstick time. "Yellow peril" scares about Asian immigration produced anti-Oriental riots in Vancouver in 1887 and again in 1907. In 1914, gunboats forced the *Komagata Maru*, with 376 Sikhs aboard, to weigh anchor and leave Vancouver harbour. Legislative discrimination against Japanese-Canadians was already entrenched in B.C. before "fifth column" frights led to their internment in the 1940s, and it was four years after World War II ended before they were allowed to return to the coast without RCMP permits. Throughout the 1950s and 1960s there were always the dreaded Communist spies, usually said to have infested B.C.'s labour unions.

Throughout the 1980s, several law-enforcement authorities across North America had become convinced that "satanic cults" were kidnapping people, brainwashing them and forcing them to participate in ritual sex, murder, and cannibalism. For some reason, the craze took root particularly well in Texas, but it was faddish in Canada as well. The news media took the stories seriously. Government agencies were mobilized, conferences were convened, social workers were conscripted, and millions of dollars were spent.

Simon Fraser University sociology professor Michael Kenny has studied the phenomenon, and he says the only explanation he has ever come across that would account for the public appeal of conspiracy theories is that they help confused people make sense of a complex world. Conspiracy proponents usually employ the simplest tactics to win converts, Kenny says, and their theories usually have a built-in defence against every criticism, a "self-confirming loop" that will sustain assaults of reason. Nothing is going to change their minds. "They're professionally educated people who go around and give workshops. They go around and propagate the most outlandish conspiracies, and people come and sit down and take notes and they buy all that stuff."

In 1995, British Columbia's future was obscured behind dark clouds. The old forests seemed to be disappearing, along with the salmon. Complex webs of trade law, park plans, court decisions, and new resource-management processes had made the province a perplexing place to live and work. Treaty talks were just another reason for otherwise intelligent people to lose their nerve and slip into paranoia. In times like these, when someone comes along with an easy explanation for everything that justifies people's worst fears, a lot of them sign up.

At the centre of B.C.'s land-claims hysteria was Melvin H. Smith, QC, retired bureaucrat, B.C. Taxpayers' Association chairman, and Reform party oracle. Smith had been busy churning out columns for *BC Report* magazine, warning of the capitulation and appeasement governments had been pursuing in their "secret" talks with Native leaders. He had just published a book, *Our Home or Native Land? What Governments' Aboriginal Policy Is Doing to Canada*, and it had become the manifesto of a growing movement in British Columbia that was united in its terror of everything B.C.'s Native leadership had fought for during the preceding hundred years. Smith had become the Canadian version of Bill Lowman, a Washington state commercial fisherman whose 1982 book, *220 Million Custers*, remained the bible of the American anti-Indian lobby. In Lowman's mind, U.S. policy "has evolved into a nationwide, sinister juggernaut, exacting from Americans sacrifices of property, money, rights and identity".

Similarly, Smith warned of "governments' actions of alarming proportions that have been quietly yet inextricably unfolding" while Canadians remained "blissfully unaware" of it all. "The map of Canada is being redrawn before our very eyes," Smith wrote, as "vast areas of the public lands of Canada are being conveyed forever to a relatively few aboriginal people. ... new and more 'governments' are springing up like mushrooms ... governments have abdicated their obligation to govern," and the plotters were covering their tracks with "federally-funded misinformation campaigns".

As the Nisga'a controversy proved, hysteria works.

Even an issue as apparently inconsequential as an Indian band's plan for a foreshore condominium development on its own reserve could degenerate into circumstances only barely above the level of a mob scene. On Canada Day 1995, more than forty protesters showed up at the Tsawwassen reserve to stage their own "roadblock". Whatever legitimate environmental worries they might have had – and, without doubt, the project raised a number of environmental questions that deserved answers – they were drowned out as organizers boasted that unlike Native roadblock participants, the protesters were not being paid by the federal government for their efforts. Carrying placards that read "One Canada – One Law", the protesters hurled insults at band members about welfare and taxes. Organizer Lynn Kemp said Delta residents were angry that the Indian band was circumventing environmental-protection rules that applied to all other Canadians and was pushing ahead a project that would house 14,000 people. It didn't seem to matter that, in fact, federal environmental assessments had been conducted and the band's Tsatsu Shores project passed its screening. A 340-unit development was approved, only 280 units were going to be built, and the project was expected to house between five hundred and nine hundred people. But talks with Delta council broke down, and the whole issue of taxation and municipal services appeared destined for the courts.

Hysteria works.

While Liberal leader Gordon Campbell hadn't avoided the chance to get in on it whenever he got a chance, it had become particularly fashionable in both federal and provincial Reform parties, and the most extravagant claims had their own built-in defences. To explain the absence of any evidence to support sinister occurrences taking place behind closed doors, all that needed to be said was that the talks were going on in secret. That was a favourite of B.C. Reform party leader Jack Weisgerber, who campaigned relentlessly on the spectre of a "veil of secrecy" shrouding treaty talks across the province, even though the B.C. government had concluded no treaty. Apart from the separate Nisga'a process, there were only a handful of treaty sessions actually underway in B.C., but they had begun only a few months prior to Weisgerber's scare stories and they were nowhere near substantive discussions. The industry-dominated, thirty-one-member Treaty Negotiation Advisory Committee enjoyed access to all the talks. The Union of B.C. Municipalities sat at the table. Local treaty advisory committees (TACs) and regional advisory committees (RACs) were in the loop. Hundreds of people were engaged in the process in one way or another. Negotiating sessions were open to the local cablevision stations. The B.C. government had made public its negotiators' instructions. Two lengthy documents set out the negotiators' mandates in treaty principles, and the government's policies in land and resources. Both the federal and provincial governments publicly contemplated treaties that would provide a larger land base for Native communities (to total an estimated five percent of the province), formal participation in land-use decisions, security of access to traditional resources, a "self-government" package, and components for economic self-sufficiency. All that these discussions had produced by the summer of 1995 were about

fifty pre-treaty "interim measures" agreements designed to keep
options open for treaty negotiators before the talks actually
began. The talks were no more secretive (actually much less so)
than the resource-management meetings between government
and industry that were taking place every day.

Nonetheless, "people's livelihoods are at stake," Weisgerber
warned. "Their jobs and businesses are in limbo."

One Reform party MP publicly speculated that Ottawa, acting
on some dark but unspecified motive, might actually be deliberately pushing the West Coast's fish stocks into extinction. Keith
Martin, the Reform MP for Esquimalt-Juan de Fuca, had become
so paranoid about the "upper echelons" in federal fisheries management that in November 1993 he said "a criminal investigation should be conducted by the RCMP to determine whether
politicians and bureaucrats have been wilfully mismanaging the
fishing industry." A group of like-minded commercial fishermen
filed suit in B.C. Supreme Court alleging that this was actually
happening. The fishermen asked for a declaration awarding them
damages for an unspecified "economic loss" they had suffered
because of a conspiracy involving then-Fisheries Minister Brian
Tobin, a former deputy minister, two assistant deputy ministers,
a former fisheries regional director-general, and a handful of
other alleged accomplices. According to their statement of claim,
Tobin and his officials, "in collusion with various aboriginal
organizations", had routinely, deliberately, and wilfully committed criminal acts. They had "condoned and encouraged" poaching. They deliberately diverted enforcement efforts to "facilitate"
poaching, "and in some cases participated" in illegal fish sales.
They diverted conservation funds to finance these covert operations, and they deliberately concealed statistics and falsified data.

In February 1994, Reform MP Jay Hill (Prince George-Peace

River) told a local newspaper that Native people were "making hundreds of millions of dollars" peddling tax-free tobacco in a cross-country enterprise that warranted mobilizing the army, if necessary, "even if it means bloodshed". In March 1995, Nanaimo-Cowichan Reform MP Bob Ringma, a retired major-general, criticized the federal budget cuts in military expenditures on the grounds that Canada would weaken its defence against Native uprisings. "I see trouble on the horizon with Native bands in Canada," he said.

Before the land-claims uproars of the 1990s, widespread paranoia had a significant impact on land-use debates in British Columbia in the late 1980s. Then, the conspirators were environmentalists bent on an "unfinishable agenda" to wreck the free-world economy, and the origin of all that paranoia was the U.S. Northwest. British Columbia's great green scare was in full flight following a legendary conference in Reno, Nevada, in the summer of 1988. The gathering was sponsored by the Centre for the Defense of Free Enterprise, an arm of the American Freedom Coalition, one of the political wings of Sun Myung Moon's Unification Church (the Moonies). It was the brainchild of anti-environmentalist crusader Ron Arnold, founder of the so-called Wise Use movement, consultant to the pesticide industry, and self-described "master of cheap shots". Arnold's pronouncements included the assertion that the environmental movement was established as "a vehicle by which the USSR can encourage the free world to voluntarily cripple its own economy".

The B.C. delegation to Reno included several Council of Forest Industries officials, Port Alberni Mayor Gillian Trumper, Port McNeill Mayor Gerry Furney, several executives from MacMillan Bloedel, plus representatives from Western Forest Products, the Truck Loggers Association, Share the Stein, and Vancouver Island's Share Our Forests group. The American delegates comprised a panorama of off-road motorcycle clubs, bow hunters, property-rights enthusiasts, snowmobile groups, forest companies and mining companies, the Citizens Equal Rights Alliance (the U.S. anti-Indian umbrella group), and the Citizens Committee for the Right to Keep and Bear Arms. They hailed from places like Hayden Lake, Idaho (home of the Aryan Nations Church), and Roswell, New Mexico (site of the famous alien-survives-UFO-crash rumpus). Arnold's main strategic advice to the forest industry was that environmentalists had to be battled by front groups funded by resource companies but with no obvious ties to resource companies. Before long, small-town B.C. was covered in yellow ribbons, the unofficial flag of the Wise Use movement. The rhetoric of the fringes quickly moved to the mainstream. Delusional backwoods characters found themselves in the company of like minded citizens in tailored suits.

A group called North Island Citizens for Shared Resources called for an "economic defence strategy" against groups like the Sierra Club, Greenpeace, and the Western Canada Wilderness Committee, which were alleged to be "dedicated to the destruction of all resource-related jobs in British Columbia". A senior MacMillan Bloedel official confided to a *Vancouver Sun* reporter that B.C.'s environmental groups were funded by "communists and neo-Nazi groups from South Africa". Socred Forests Minister Dave Parker remarked: "One of the best ways to get economic chaos in North America is to stymie development. One of the best ways to stymie development is get a preservationist environmental movement going."

Invigorated by the issue of race, the 1990s land-claims rhetoric was every bit as strident, and the imagined conspiracies were comic-book perfect. The subversive exploits that Smith catalogues in *Our Home or Native Land?* were the handiwork of what he described as a shadowy "Indian industry" of Native lawyers, academics, consultants, and advisers – all funded by government – in league with "overzealous bureaucrats and compliant politicians". (I should confess that I might qualify as having once been linked with this conspiracy. After I left the *Vancouver Sun*, when I wasn't writing for the *Georgia Straight* or writing books, I worked on research contracts for aboriginal groups, and spent six months as an analyst with the B.C. Treaty Commission. I was "blissfully unaware" of any plots underway around me.)

Although Melvin H. Smith's name appears on the book's cover, Smith acknowledged that *Our Home or Native Land?* is really more of a collaborative effort. The book was built around Smith's memoirs of his career as a constitutional adviser to the B.C. government, which started in the 1960s under W. A. C. Bennett. Smith continued to enjoy influence until about a year after Bill Vander Zalm moved into the premier's office, when Smith appears to have been relegated to a basement office somewhere near the legislative precinct. Although Smith maintains that he enjoyed a splendid career until the end, nobody in government appears to have been particularly interested in his theories during the Vander Zalm years, and in Smith's book, this is the point in B.C.'s history where everything begins to go terribly wrong. Smith's co-authors were: Steve Vanagas, a former Social Credit activist who also wrote for *BC Report*; the Fisheries Survival Coalition, the alliance of anti-Native alarmists in the fishing industry; and Norman Mullins, the lawyer who turned heads in 1993 with a letter to the Canadian Bar Association's national newsletter protesting the "absurd and unacceptable claims, demands, threats, and lies of Indians in Canada." Research on the Prairie treaties was provided not by, say, the Native-studies department of the University of Lethbridge but by the Canadian Taxpayers' Federation, from which even Alberta Premier Ralph Klein recoiled. Vancouver chat-show host Rafe Mair wrote a glowing foreword.

As the title *Our Home or Native Land?* implies, Smith and his friends could not foresee a future that was anything more than one or the other, us or them, all or nothing. According to Smith, everything about aboriginal rights and land claims was wrong. It was an elaborate, legally unsound construction that promoted "rights based on race" when the real solution to the complex and daunting land-claims mess was actually so simple, anybody could understand it. All we needed to do was take whatever "modest aboriginal interest" that remained after 130 years of white settlement and have it "discharged", preferably by the federal government alone. If Native people wanted settlements, they would first have to submit to the precondition that whatever constitutionally protected aboriginal rights they still had would have to be surrendered so they could be forever "extinguished". After that, they could have provincially chartered municipalities if they wanted, but no "visual pollution, i.e. third party roadside billboards", or they could just sell their reserves. They would be just like everybody else, and then everything would be okay.

Instead, Smith said, both Ottawa and Victoria were pursuing solutions to outstanding Native issues that went far beyond what the courts had provided regarding Native rights and government obligations, and their "politically correct" agenda threatened to permanently entrench apartheid in Canada's Constitution.

It's a theory that was particularly popular during Smith's tour with the Reform party's cross-province "town hall" meetings on land claims. The theory had become accepted as gospel in Reform party circles. Rafe Mair and *Vancouver Sun* columnists Gordon Gibson and Trevor Lautens had all enthusiastically endorsed Smith's remedies.

But a closer look at Smith's book shows that the court decisions he cited as evidence that his plans would work don't actually say what he claimed. Provincial Court Judge Cunliffe Barnett described Smith's arguments as little more than "Reform party positions dressed up as legal scholarship".

Smith claimed that his arguments come from the 1991 B.C. Supreme Court decision by Chief Justice Alan McEachern in the Gitksan-Wet'suwet'en land-claims lawsuit known as Delgamuukw v. the Queen. He also pointed to the 1993 B.C. Appeal Court decision in Delgamuukw, one of eight aboriginal-rights decisions the Appeal Court released simultaneously. In some cases, the rulings themselves, and the words of the judges who wrote them, directly contradict what Smith claimed their judgments were about. And Smith completely ignored Supreme Court of Canada findings that would render unconstitutional the postures he said the government should adopt.

Overall, the 1993 rulings provided a mix of findings, sometimes in the Natives' favour and sometimes not. More than a dozen judges were involved in the trials as they made their way through the court system. Judge Barnett was one of the "majority opinion" judges involved in the cases – he was the presiding judge in the Alphonse case (a charge of illegal hunting laid against Shuswap hunter Dennis Alphonse) – and his finding in that case was upheld unanimously by the B.C. Court of Appeal. Barnett described Smith's theories this way: "Whatever Mr. Smith's impeccable constitutional credentials might be, these are all views that you can read in *BC Report* magazine, and that's where they belong. He really shouldn't camouflage things like this and he shouldn't misrepresent the decisions as badly as he does. He's distorting some of these decisions so badly ... he is using all the old excuses. The legal landscape concerning Native people in British Columbia has changed."

Vancouver Sun columnist Gordon Gibson seemed as unaware of the changed landscape as Smith was. "Our governments are close to setting a 'politically correct' variety of racism into constitutional concrete," Gibson wrote. "Mel Smith's warning blows the lid off a developing tragedy of our time."

In the US Northwest, hysteria had run so deep in the

1980s that entire communities were imagining occult plots within their own federal government. They were staging armed confrontations with federal officials. They were passing illegal county ordinances declaring ownership of federal lands. When they weren't assembling armouries of assault weapons, they were organizing trailer-park film nights to watch secret videotapes of Russian tanks rumbling through the deep woods of Alabama. Like their counterparts in British Columbia, the hill people of Washington, Idaho, and Montana had made common cause with well-heeled, urban corporate executives. They enjoyed enormous success trouncing Democrats at the polls. Alliances like People for the West and the National Coalition for Public Lands and Natural Resources maintained a legislative agenda that proposed to gut the Endangered Species Act, dismantle wilderness designations, and write mine-friendly pollution control laws, and by the mid-1990s they were well on their way.

The B.C. Mining Association was one of the leading hard-lin-

ers on the B.C. government's thirty-one-member Treaty Negotiation Advisory Committee. The association, prior to B.C.'s 1996
provincial elections, prepared a "political action plan", developed a database with the names and addresses of the 30,000 B.C.
residents involved in the mining economy, and prepared a "voters' guide" and other initiatives. Barbara Grannell, executive
director of the National Coalition for Public Lands and Natural
Resources, delivered the keynote address at the mining association's 1995 symposium on B.C.'s land-use conflicts. She told the
delegates: "There isn't a lot of difference between Canada and
the United States, or any country where the green lobby has a
foothold, when it comes to the elitist, socialist environmental
agenda." Grannell did not mince words about what B.C.'s mining industry was best advised to mobilize voters against: "The
politics of socialism. ... It is the politics that brainwashes the
masses into believing it's all for their own good. The politics that
reinforces the value of animals and nature above the value of the
individual."

U.S. writer Margaret L. Knox, who investigated the phenomenon of anti-Indian paranoia for the Fund for Constitutional Government, the *Los Angeles Times*, the Smithsonian, and *Sierra*
magazine, said British Columbia was just getting a taste of what
it's like when fringe ideologies move closer to the mainstream.
"You get these largely uneducated rural white people, and a lot
of sophisticated corporate guys get them blaming environmentalists. If you're in a citizens' militia, you blame the federal government for everything. If you live near a reservation, you blame the
tribal authorities. Usually, these are all the same people. It's a
stew of anti-Indian, anti-environmentalist, anti-government
stuff, and they talk about global conspiracies, the whole thing."
Knox noted that British Columbia's anti-Native rhetoric, with its

secret land giveaways, government-funded "misinformation campaigns," cover-ups, and "rights based on race" was a linguistic photocopy of the language employed by the American anti-Indian lobby.

The anti-Indian lobby used a "creative nomenclature" designed to provide an appearance of respect for equality and civil rights, Knox said. Montana had its All Citizens Equal, North Dakota had the Committee for Equality, Minnesota had its Totally Equal Americans, and their umbrella group was the Montana-based Citizens Equal Rights Alliance. By 1995, B.C. was home to another group with an egalitarian-sounding name: BCFIRE, or British Columbians for Individual Rights and Equality. Nanaimo had its All Citizens Equal, which was circulating petitions and writing letters to newspapers: "Natives are asking for all the Crown lands in B.C. ... if the NDP succeeds in giving away this great province, what will you tell your children and their children after them?" In Montana, Citizens Equal Rights Alliance spokesman John Cramer lamented: "I thought the U.S. was about coming together. What we're doing here is promoting another Yugoslavia." The *Vancouver Sun*'s Trevor Lautens warned: "Canada isn't Yugoslavia. ... Do you think that people nostalgic with age-old tribal memories of life before the white man have forgotten their even older quarrels and competition with other tribes, newly broadened?"

Lautens was one of Melvin H. Smith's biggest fans, calling him "a constitutional lawyer of the first rank" who "probably has more experience with constitutional matters than any other living British Columbian". If this was so, Smith's experience had not been an entirely pleasant one. Over the course of a

quarter century, Canada passed over Smith's constitutional proposals, one after the other. There was his plan to render the
House of Commons subservient to an all-powerful Senate, com-
posed exclusively of provincially elected senators with "absolute
veto" over some federal decisions and a "suspensive veto" over
everything else. One of his proposals was to head off the Charter
of Rights with two bills of rights, one for Canada and one for the
provinces, with politicians bound by neither. Things had not
exactly gone his way. In 1982, the Constitution was finally patri-
ated and proclaimed as the Constitution Act, with its Charter of
Rights. To make matters worse for Smith's view of the way
things should be, Section 35 of the Constitution Act states: "The
existing aboriginal and treaty rights of the aboriginal peoples of
Canada are hereby recognized and affirmed." To make it even
clearer for people, Section 35 defines "aboriginal" as Indian,
Inuit, and Métis, and the word "treaty" is defined to mean future
treaties as well.

Smith was given to much hand-wringing about how the country could have adopted a constitution that protected Native
rights against federal and provincial politicians. "Such is the box
that Canadians have been placed in through the acquiescence of
their political leadership," Smith wrote. He was baffled by it all,
and he speculated that the federal government and the country's
ten premiers didn't understand what they were doing because the
provision was so "highly technical". Unfortunately, the
"prospects look dim" for Section 35's removal, Smith concluded,
because it probably would have been unconstitutional to force
such an act upon the country's Native people.

Section 35 wasn't Canada's first mistake, Smith said.

In 1969, the federal government unveiled its ill-advised
"White Paper", which proposed to phase out existing treaties,

abolish all references to Native people in law, and absolve Canada of any legislative responsibility for Native people. Smith reckoned this was a good idea. It also came close to provoking insurrections across the country, and Ottawa ditched it without fanfare less than a year later.

But Smith would have had us turn back the clock even further. In 1951, the federal government dropped its prohibition against Native people raising funds to push land claims. Under that law, enacted in 1927, Native people could not hire lawyers to represent them in land disputes. Smith proposed to revive this prohibition in a different form to head off treaty-entitlement cases and old reserve-land disputes, by arming governments with a kind of statute-of-limitations defence. "It is no coincidence that our jurisprudence has established strict time limits and other evidenciary rules that determine whether claims are legitimate," Smith writes. "No other class of Canadians is similarly privileged either in the courts or in their dealings with government." As for Native attempts to address these unresolved grievances outside the courtroom, Smith said that shouldn't be allowed either. Disputes of this sort, handled mainly through the federal specific-claims process, were just another example of federal "largesse" that should be halted: "Savings of further hundreds of millions of dollars would result."

But it is not as though nothing had gone Smith's way. It was Smith who helped Bill Bennett champion the "No" side during a series of constitutional conferences in the 1980s that Native leaders had hoped would result in a negotiated constitutional compromise on self-government. But after Vander Zalm was elected, Smith's glory days were over.

Vander Zalm recognized early in his term that times were changing. The government was engaged in numerous court bat-

tles against Natives, and judges were increasingly coming down
on the Native side. Most of the court disputes arose from the fact
that no treaties were signed west of the Rockies, except for the
fourteen colonial documents in force on southern Vancouver
Island that judges had to continually instruct the B.C. government to obey. B.C.'s old position on the "Indian land question",
which hadn't changed much since the 1870s, was best expressed
by former Attorney General Brian Smith when he said a B.C.
decision to join with Ottawa in treaty talks would be to go "the
Neville Chamberlain route". In later years, after he had left politics, Brian Smith had the grace to concede the error of his earlier
conclusions.

Not Melvin H. Smith. The Vander Zalm government had
abandoned the old line, deciding that B.C.'s interests could best
be safeguarded by full and active participation with the federal
government in land-claims settlements. The move was welcomed
by B.C.'s mainline Native leaders (Ottawa had been waiting for
B.C. to get to the table for years), and the new policy enjoyed
widespread popular support. But not from Smith, who described
the move as "capitulation". If nothing else, Smith was consistent
in his public postures, although it wasn't clear how he justified
his leadership of the B.C. Taxpayers' Association (which campaigned against union-wage laws, too-rich welfare packets, and
generous public-service pensions) while he himself was drawing
a $60,000 annual public-service pension ever since his last year
on the public payroll, when he drew a salary of about $100,000.
Meanwhile, the treaty process that Mair, Lautens, the *Province*'s
Brian Kieran, and the rest had cast as a Great Leap Forward by
wild-eyed, farm-selling, down-the-river-sending, white-guilt-rid-
den New Democrats was actually invented under Social Credit
while Reform leader Jack Weisgerber was Vander Zalm's Native

Affairs minister. And the confidentiality rules that applied to third-party advisers in the Nisga'a talks, so roundly condemned by the B.C. Reform party, were actually established during Weisgerber's tenure.

But back to Smith.

It is March 11, 1991, three days after Judge McEachern handed down his decision in Delgamuukw. In the legislature, Socred and NDP MLAs join in a rare show of unanimity behind the government's response when Attorney General Russ Fraser says: "Let's not consider this a win-lose situation, but an opportunity. The government is committed to working with Natives throughout the province to resolve their legitimate differences."

Smith wrote that he was disgusted by Fraser's "weasel words", reckoning that the McEachern judgment should have had a "profound effect" on federal and provincial policy, but "alas, the decision was largely ignored." In fact, the only matter of substance that ended up being ignored in McEachern's decision was his finding that there had been a blanket extinguishment of aboriginal rights in B.C. prior to Confederation. One compelling reason it was ignored is that it was unanimously overturned by the B.C. Appeal Court two years later.

What the government could not immediately ignore was McEachern's finding that despite the supposed extinguishment of constitutionally protected aboriginal rights, the B.C. government, like the federal government, was burdened by a "legally enforceable fiduciary duty" to Native peoples. McEachern ordered B.C. to behave in a non-adversarial manner toward Native people, and he granted Natives a "right of consultation" in land-use decisions — not necessarily a veto, but Native consent and agreement was "much to be desired", the judge said. McEachern's instructions were spelled out in eight pages of the decision. The fiduciary duty – which survived the appeal, and consequently bound B.C. thereafter – effectively forced Victoria to consult and negotiate with Natives over every imaginable provincially sanctioned activity that might potentially interfere with aboriginal activities. Never before did the idea of treaties make better sense.

In Smith's *Our Home or Native Land?*, there is only passing reference to the fiduciary duty that bound the B.C. government. McEachern described his own ruling as a "divided success" for both sides. Smith called the McEachern judgment an "unqualified victory" over the Native position. Smith applied the same kind of treatment to the Supreme Court of Canada's 1990 Sparrow decision. The Sparrow decision provided a step-by-step elaboration of the restraints that had to be placed, much to this country's embarrassment, on political interference in the constitutional rights of Native people. The point of Section 35 of the Constitution, the judges explained, was to impose a "measure of control over government conduct and a strong check on legislative power". Smith wrote off the Sparrow decision as simply an "event to further complicate DFO's deteriorating management efforts" that was otherwise "narrow in its legal import".

But it was the commitment by Ottawa and Victoria to acknowledge the "inherent" aboriginal right of self-government in treaty talks that caused Smith to pray: "May God deliver us from such folly!" (In his spare time, Smith, an evangelical Christian, gave church workshops on the legal implications of St. Paul's epistles.) "Both the B.C. Supreme Court and the B.C. Court of Appeal [in the Delgamuukw decisions] turned the proposition down flat." In fact, all that the judges "turned down flat" was the idea that self-government is the scary, sovereign-jurisdiction kind that Smith asked God to protect us from. The

Delgamuukw decision acknowledged that Canadian law had already assigned government jurisdictions to Ottawa and the provinces, but it confirmed the aboriginal right to internal self-rule – so the challenge was to ensure that Native and non-Native governments "co-exist". When Judge Alan McFarlane wrote the majority findings in the Delgamuukw decision, he said: "The establishment of some form of Indian self-government beyond the regulatory powers delegated by the Indian Act is ripe for negotiation and reconciliation."

Reconciliation and co-existence were cards that just didn't appear in Smith's deck. Instead, he called for a purge of the "underlying sense of collective guilt visited upon non-Native Canadians" and a quick judicial reference to the courts on whether B.C. should have been involved in these sorts of discussions at all. Smith conceded that the Supreme Court of Canada ordered Ottawa to behave in a fiduciary, "non-adversarial" manner toward Native people, but he held this up as evidence that Ottawa couldn't be trusted to serve the public interest in treaty talks. It was the heart of Smith's entire theory. You couldn't serve the "public interest" and still behave in a "non-adversarial" manner toward Native people. The "Native interest" and the "public interest" were irreconcilable and hopelessly opposed. It was us or them, our way or the highway. It was either Our Home or Native Land.

Even the B.C. Appeal Court's Delgamuukw decision – which Smith held up as the proof of his positions – directly contradicted this view. Judge McFarlane explicitly rejected what he himself called the "all or nothing" approach, calling for a "co-existence approach" instead.

Smith was undaunted. To protect the public interest against Native people and their collaborators within government, Smith

proposed an all-powerful, provincially appointed "Treaty Ombudsman", effectively unanswerable to the government in power.
The ombudsman would serve a ten-year term and could not be
recalled except by a unanimous vote of the legislature or a
provincial referendum. He would enjoy "unfettered access" to
treaty talks to ensure the "public interest" was being served, and
could put any and all aspects of a treaty to a public referendum
(i.e., grant the nearest white settlement a veto). Sort of like a
viceroy from the olden days. It was difficult not to suspect that
Smith imagined himself in such a position: a ten-year stint, parad-
ing in a flag-festooned limousine from Kelowna to Osoyoos,
descending in his helicopter upon Smithers or Kispiox, dispens-
ing advice to rural ideologues, signing copies of his book, ordering a referendum here, instructing appreciative mayors there, and
having his photo snapped among the colourful tribesmen. But the
hardest part of the job would have been figuring out when to
invoke the "public interest" to impose limits upon whatever aboriginal or treaty rights were being considered. Smith didn't say
how to deal with this dilemma. Fortunately, the Supreme Court
of Canada had already fairly laughed the idea out of court in its
unanimous 1990 Sparrow decision. The judges found that "the
'public interest' justification is so vague as to provide no mean-
ingful guidance and so broad as to be unworkable as a test for the
justification of a limitation on constitutional rights."

It probably wouldn't have come up anyway. Smith's precondi-
tions for treaty negotiations effectively guaranteed that they
wouldn't even happen. Smith said he would have instructed government negotiators to concede nothing more than his own version of what the courts had already ordered governments to
concede. And no Native community would have been allowed at
the table without agreeing that whatever other "undefined abo-

riginal interests" they might have had required "extinguishment … as a condition of entering into land claim agreements".

Whatever their exotic customs and traditions, B.C.'s Native leaders, in their century of struggle for treaties, have never done anything that would lead us to believe they would be willing to form up in lines to surrender all their aboriginal rights in return for the privilege of having people like Mel Smith lecture them about unsightly billboards.

It's not going to happen.

During an unusually off-the-deep-end radio show in June 1995, Rafe Mair endorsed Smith's agenda, and he said the best policy was for Ottawa and Victoria to "go back to square one". Square one was five years earlier, before Vander Zalm, in Smith's view, "capitulated" to Native leaders and agreed to join in treaty negotiations. That summer there were Native blockades at Alert Bay, Agassiz, Fountain, Gitwangak, Kitwancool, Meziadin Junction, Moricetown, New Aiyansh, North Vancouver, Oliver, Pavilion, Pemberton, Penticton, Toosey, and Vernon. And Oka.

By 1995, it looked certain that maybe nightstick time was coming again. In the 124 summers that had passed since British Columbia entered Confederation, the politicians of this province had not once demonstrated that they had the backbone for the difficult work of negotiation and reconciliation with Native people. In 1990, all of us said we were finally going to get around to the job. By 1995, as spring was turning to summer, civil discourse was collapsing into the headlines and the sound bites and the slogans of populist barbarism. It was the middle of the night, and Native "militants" were setting up roadblocks on the Douglas Lake Road in the Nicola Valley and on the Adams Lake

Road northeast of Kamloops. The issues had become too complicated for the newspaper columnists to explain. It had become a simple matter of referring to the appropriate sections of Melvin H. Smith's manifesto to show how wrong everyone had been five years before, when we made our promises.

We would see why we had to crush their petty rebellions whenever they arose, and we would know there was no cause to feel guilty about ourselves. We had no duty to these people. We could give them such a thrashing as to be a spectacle unto the world.

The Circus Comes to Gustafsen Lake

Long before the circus came to 100 Mile House, when it was still possible to sort out the difference between what was real and what was invented, there were two men. One was Percy Rosette. The other was Lyall James. They had a disagreement that got a little out of hand.

Lyall James was a rancher from Dog Creek, a white man, not a particularly worldly person, not exceptionally quick on his feet. Percy Rosette was a quiet, introverted man. A Shuswap, Rosette lived on the fringes of his community, the village of Alkali Lake. It's not like Rosette and James were friends or anything, but before it all started, they always got along fine.

Years before, Alkali Lake was a desolate place. Many of its children had suffered sexual abuse at the St. Joseph's residential school in Williams Lake, and they brought the disease home with them. Death and suicide were endemic there through the 1970s. But Alkali Lake went on to become an inspiration to Native communities throughout the country because of its success in breaking the cycle of hopelessness that had befallen so many of them. The people relied on their own resources and their own spiritual traditions and became one of the first truly "dry" communities in the Chilcotin-Cariboo country.

Percy Rosette was one of the redeemed. By the mid-1980s, he had become enthralled with the sundance tradition, a spiritual discipline that emerged in the late 1800s among the messianic cults and apocalyptic movements that were occurring throughout the plains and the western plateau. The sundance was revived in the 1970s, a time of "Indian militancy". It became associated with the self-discovery and self-improvement movements that have proved so successful as remedies to the chronic alcoholism, substance abuse, and violence so many Native communities have struggled to defeat. Over the years, Percy Rosette had become convinced that an area overlooking Gustafsen Lake, a popular fishing spot in the Cariboo region, was spiritually charged, that it was an important, sacred place of the type routinely identified in visions by sundance devotees.

Rosette talked to James about it. Rosette said he wanted to use the site for sundance ceremonies during the summer. There was something important about the place, in a spiritual way. It was the kind of thing James wasn't going to understand easily, but, as it is with all of us, there were a lot of things in the world that James didn't understand. James told Rosette he could do what he wanted, as long as the sundance people didn't impede access by hunters and anglers at the lake, and as long as he didn't construct any permanent structures.

That was fine. It was a straightforward agreement between two men. That was in 1988.

The way *100 Mile House Free Press* editor Steven Frasher explained it, there was never any real trouble associated with the sundancers. Percy Rosette and the handful of sundance devotees kept mainly to themselves, camping at a site they were convinced was one of the most important places on the earth's spiritual landscape, with a "sacred arbour" and a "sacred burial ground" revealed to them in visions. Rosette had a small following among some local Shuswap families from communities like Canim Lake and Alkali Lake. Many of them were disenchanted with the local band leadership and the Cariboo Tribal Council, and Gustafsen Lake became a place where people talked around the campfire about their "sellout" leaders. But Percy and his group kept mainly to themselves, and most of the local Natives wanted nothing to do with Percy and his ceremonies anyway.

By 1990, word about Gustafsen Lake had spread to the scattered followers of the sundance tradition throughout Western Canada and the United States. It came to be regarded as one of those "power" sites that emerge on the landscape, suitable for important sundance ceremonies over a four-year cycle, after which the "power" is said to move on to another site. Percy Rosette was earning a bit of a name for himself. He described himself as "keeper of the faith" at Gustafsen Lake. Other than that, Rosette wasn't causing any trouble.

From time to time, there were instances of "cultural wires getting crossed", Frasher said. Every year, as July approached, the sundancers' fervour grew more intense. Percy and his "traditional war chief", Ernie Archie, would approach anglers and campers and warn them of the physical danger they were courting by their proximity to the sacred site. Archie could be a bit disconcerting in his manner. Hunters and anglers did not like these encounters. To the ranching community and the white community around 100 Mile House, Gustafsen Lake was becoming the focus for all the suspicions and concerns that non-Native British Columbians harboured about Native people and Native land claims generally. Rosette and his followers, in turn, were becoming paranoid about the outside world and increasingly mistrustful of the local Native leadership. But there was nothing that could conclusively confirm any "white" suspicions, and then in 1992 there were reports of shots fired at Gustafsen Lake. Close to the sundance camp, a tent occupied by non-Native campers was struck by several rounds.

These were times when it was still possible to know what was really happening at Gustafsen Lake. There was no police perimeter. There was no crush of media crews. There was just the local newspaper in 100 Mile House, doing its best to report the plain facts about things that happened. After everything that followed, the straightest, cleanest, most useful coverage of the debacle that Gustafsen Lake became could not be found in the files of the *Vancouver Sun*, the *Province*, or the *Globe and Mail*, and it would not be seen in the archives of the CBC or BCTV or U.TV. It can be found in a handful of articles written by Steven Frasher and his small crew of staffers at the *Free Press*. Frasher remains the only reporter who wandered the site with Rosette and asked sundancers honest questions. The pages of this forty-year-old newspaper were the only place where you could have found some reliable answers to the most important question about the disgraceful spectacle that developed up there. It is the only question the big news organizations could never fully address, because they just cover the news conferences, and, besides, they weren't even there. The question is "Why?"

Usually, the answers are pretty straightforward, as the facts behind the 1992 gunshots show. Frasher describes the 1992 incident as "something like one of those house parties where a bunch of bikers show up". As for the gunshots, there are always gunshots. This is the Cariboo. As it turned out, these shots were fired by "just some goofs shooting at some gophers or something". But the gunshots heightened tensions in the area. Local non-Natives were becoming increasingly concerned about the sundancers, the local Canim Lake band made it clear to anyone who asked that they wanted nothing to do with Rosette and his group, and the sundancers started to take on the kind of attitudes one would expect from a ragged band of outcasts.

Nevertheless, the 1993 ceremonies came and went without incident. Gustafsen Lake was becoming associated in Native communities with a kind of romantic militancy, but the 1994 ceremonies also came and went without anything more uproarious than Ernie Archie's usual bravado and the resulting nervousness among visiting anglers.

Lyall James had been assuming that 1994 was the end of the sundance "cycle" at Gustafsen Lake, and given the reputation Rosette and his followers had established for themselves, he was happy to be rid of them. Rosette, meanwhile, had been travelling widely, visiting far-flung communities and meeting more sundancers and the movement's alienated, often violent hangers-on. In his travels, Rosette had also become acquainted with Bruce Clark, a bombastic white lawyer who had developed a notorious reputation for himself among Native lawyers and the mainstream Native leadership. His notoriety was equalled only by his cultlike following among certain groups of Native "dissidents" and white radicals across Canada. Clark decried "sellout" Native leaders. He had been known to accuse judges of "treason" and "genocide". He routinely engaged in courtroom outbursts. He also lost case after case, failing, time and again, to advance his peculiar aboriginal-rights theories, which involve assertions of Native sovereignty and Native immunity from law enforcement. Clark's posturing found fertile ground among sundancers.

Meanwhile, a parallel form of extremism had been taking root among many non-Natives across British Columbia. The long-overdue process of treaty negotiations in the province had just begun, and a widespread paranoia, fanned mainly by the Reform party of British Columbia, was producing its own siege mentality. While Clark had his visions of "treasonous" and "genocidal" government policy, Reformers were having their own visions and promoting their own peculiar aboriginal-rights theories. Indians were claiming "110 percent of the province"; a politically correct NDP government was forwarding a secret agenda of "rights based on race" and kowtowing to Native leaders instead of insisting that there should be "one law for all Canadians".

While the treaty process was sputtering and stumbling its way across the landscape, the NDP government was working over-time, to no great effect, trying to convince a panicked public that the government was being appropriately tough in its dealings with Native people. The only set of talks approaching conclusion were negotiations with the Nisga'a of northwestern B.C., which were being sabotaged by Reform party "leaks" of tentative treaty deals and dire warnings about "social unrest" and "violence" among angry rural white people. Throughout the Cariboo, there was a widespread fear among ranchers about what treaty negotiations might mean to their grazing leases. Despite the Cariboo Tribal Council's repeated denials, the rumour persisted that private ranch land, like Lyall James's place, was going to end up on the treaty table.

It was in this kind of overcharged climate that Lyall James, in the spring of 1995, found that Rosette had not left the ranch after all and, in fact, had been living in a remote supply cabin on ranch property all winter. And by early summer, Rosette and a handful of followers were back at their sundance site, which James apparently presumed they would have vacated after the 1994 ceremonies.

Until June 13, 1995, there was little that might have been said of the "sacred ground" of Gustafsen Lake except that it was a place where a handful of arguably paranoid Native eccentrics had perhaps overstayed their welcome on a privately owned ranch. There was some talk about the ranch itself being within an old reserve that somehow had been expropriated and converted to private ranch land, but nobody had produced any evidence that might support any legitimate claim or grievance. The sundance people were at odds with the Native communities of the area and had alienated local ranchers, anglers, and hunters, many of whom had become a bit paranoid themselves about Native people, what with Native roadblocks going up and down elsewhere in the province and all the talk making the rounds about "secret" land-claims talks.

June 13 changed everything.

The sundancers had built a fence around the site, enclosing an area of about two square kilometres. It was a breach of the agreement James and Rosette had made between themselves in 1988. Rosette had promised that access would not be impeded and no permanent structures would be built. Later, the sundancers said the fence was necessary to keep cattle off the sacred grounds. Whatever the case, James and Rosette weren't getting along anymore.

James obtained an eviction notice against Rosette and his

entourage. Rosette and his followers responded by trotting out Bruce Clark's rhetoric about unceded hunting grounds and the treachery of judges.

It is by no means clear why James and his cowboys did not simply leave the matter of the unwanted and defiant tenants to the RCMP, but on June 13, about a dozen of James's cowboys descended upon the sundancers at their camp, kicked down a door, removed a cookstove they said had been removed from a cattle camp, and allegedly defiled sundance regalia by impaling an eviction notice on a "sacred" staff. Later, one of the cowboys ("in a drunken stupor," according to a sundance news release) rode back into the sundance camp, snapping a bullwhip and warning the sundancers that the ranchers and the RCMP were mobilizing against them and the sundance camp was going to be burned out, adding: "They're all coming to get you." News of the cowboys' brave charge on the camp quickly spread through the countryside. It was all so very exciting.

Rather than run away in fright, the sundancers decided to hold firm and lay in wait for the presumed attack. Word went quickly from the camp to its far-flung supporters that an epic, Oka-like showdown was imminent.

The next day, forest-service worker George Ostoforoff and a colleague were driving a ministry vehicle along a dirt road in the vicinity of the camp, and Ostoforoff said that he saw a group of masked men along a fence line, then a plume of dust on the road ahead. Ostoforoff reckoned one of the men had fired a bullet at the road from a high-calibre rifle.

Ostoforoff wasted no time telling everybody about the incident. He reported it to the RCMP, he talked to news reporters, and he wondered aloud about why Native people are treated differently and why there isn't one law for all Canadians. Within days, Ostoforoff's questions were being raised in the provincial legislature by Reform party MLA Len Fox, who claimed that an unnamed Reform party member "familiar with the incident" had revealed to him that the RCMP was refusing, for some unknown reason, to act on Ostoforoff's complaint. Fox said: "It's a sad day when a government employee is actually shot at, presumably by militant Natives, and the RCMP doesn't lift a finger." When Attorney General Colin Gabelmann and the local RCMP detachment refuted Fox's allegations, the Reform MLA's defence was that he was just trying to make the point that there should be "one law for all British Columbians".

It didn't matter that the event, according to Steven Frasher's investigations, was simply a matter of some young idiot playing tough and goofing around. It didn't matter that the Canoe Creek Indian band and the Cariboo Tribal Council were publicly pleading with the white people to calm down and pleading with the sundancers to leave the territory "immediately" before things got out of hand. It didn't matter anymore that the RCMP, the Forests Ministry, and Lyall James were telling everyone who cared to listen that Natives and non-Natives in the area generally got along, and that this thing at Gustafsen Lake had nothing to do with land claims or aboriginal rights or anything of the sort.

Fox's alarums spread the word about Gustafsen Lake ever farther afield, exciting extremists on both sides of the ideological divide. Within days, Rosette and his "war chief", Ernie Archie, were enjoying the company of such characters as an Adams Lake Shuswap who went by the name of Wolverine and a Mohawk with a serious criminal record and the unlikely name of Splitting The Sky. There were others assembling with firearms at Gustafsen Lake. The people there were now calling themselves "The Defenders of the Shuswap Nation", although it was not clear just how many of the group by this time were even Shuswap people. The camp was swelling with non-Native supporters as well, mainly new-age white activists who volunteered to act as "communications" workers, camp cooks, witnesses to the events that would inevitably unfold, and the like. This, too, was all very exciting.

In early August, Ernie Archie was arrested for fishing during a closure on the Fraser River, near the Gang Ranch bridge. Although Archie was released, a man who was with him – Samuel David Pena – was not. Found in Pena's vehicle were semiautomatic weapons, a machine pistol, and garotte wire. The Ostoforoff business had already elevated Gustafsen Lake to a higher, stranger plane, and everything was becoming very serious. Increasingly, local non-Natives were calling for swift armed action against the sundancers. Radio hot-line shows were buzzing with it. Everybody seemed to want quick, brutal retribution.

What finally caused the situation to degenerate into a hopelessly polarized, armed standoff was a comedy of errors that unfolded on Friday, August 18. The people inside the camp (already given to apocalyptic visions at the best of times) began to imagine figures moving in the woods around them. There were noises coming through the trees. Surely this was the moment of the final battle. Panic set in. Rosette claimed he called the RCMP by cellular telephone, demanding protection because the woods were crawling with people who were coming against them, and that he and his friends would be forced to defend themselves if the camp were attacked. On the other end of the line, the RCMP staff member knew what Rosette was talking about. The noises in the woods were RCMP members sneaking through the trees, conducting a surveillance operation. He couldn't tell Rosette, and when he dismissed Rosette's complaints, Rosette became even more paranoid. One of the group aimed a weapon at a man approaching through the trees and fired. He missed. It was a Mountie.

The following day, the RCMP set the stage for the siege they were preparing to establish around Gustafsen Lake. Their plans, and their posture, were explained at a news conference in Williams Lake, where RCMP Staff Sergeant Len Olfert described the sundancers as "terrorists".

It is about this point that the real story ends, because media events are not stories that have beginnings, that have reasons, that have history. The tents go up and it becomes impossible to sort things out. It becomes impossible to calm things down. There were armoured personnel carriers roaring down dusty Cariboo back roads. School buses were carrying children past scary-looking checkpoints. There were armed men, each suffering varying degrees of testosterone poisoning. There were breathtaking skirmishes. There was panic and there were news conferences. There was Ovide Mercredi, whose very presence ensured the affair would rocket from the realm of low-level blockheadedness, where it began and belonged, to the realm of national controversy, where it could never be resolved. There was the preposterous shaven-headed Bruce Clark, descending from the sky in a helicopter like some lawyer from another planet. His strange refrain was, "Take me to your leader; I must see the Queen," and his instructions to his gun-toting clients were that they were acting within their rights to resist "genocidal police conduct".

There was the fat white man who rolled up to the police checkpoint in a white stretch limousine with a gift of dog food for the dogs he'd heard were going without food behind the lines. There was the shocking report that sundancers had assaulted Lyall James's house, firing several rounds through his window (actually, it was a sundancer's house that got shot up, fifty miles away in Lac La Hache). There was the television reporter whose main investigative contribution was his effort to determine whether the militants were on welfare, so he could rely on that always necessary shred of truth in order to describe Gustafsen Lake as yet another case of taxpayers' dollars funding outrageous Indian activity. There was the Salvation Army, bringing food for the people and prayers for the forgiveness of sins and hope for the redemption of us all.

But it is a slim hope, because there are little, venial sins in this, · and there are mortal sins, and there are sins that cry out to heaven for vengeance, and when it was all over, the cameras were already headed somewhere else. The circus tents were taken down. The RCMP musical ride left, along with the Indian desperados, the weird bald lawyer, and all the other sad little midway freaks that made the 6 o'clock news so interesting for a few weeks in the summer of 1995. There were arrests, and there was much angry talk. Thankfully, nobody got killed. And when it was all over, the people of Alkali Lake and Canim Lake and Lac La Hache and 100 Mile House and Dog Creek were left to consider some of the things they might have said about each other in the excitement of the moment, when there were television cameras around and things were not quite real. They will forgive one another, or they will not forgive one another. And if they survive the rituals we subject people to when these kinds of things happen, there will be an elderly man named Percy Rosette, of Alkali Lake, and an elderly man named Lyall James, of Dog Creek, who had a disagreement once that got a bit out of hand.

Last Day in Alexis Creek

His last day in Alexis Creek began on a warm and sunny Chilcotin morning. Spring had stayed late, and it had been a rainy summer, so all the meadows and cattle pastures of the Chilcotin Valley were lush and green. From Lee's Corner to Bull Canyon, the hay fields and alfalfa fields were scattered with round bales and square bales, and a second crop was coming up all around them. On that morning, Cunliffe Barnett strode into the Alexis Creek Community Hall on Anaham's Meadow Road dressed in a blue blazer, shirt and tie, blue slacks, and grey cowboy boots. He didn't look his sixty years, and there was nothing in his arrival that day that would have led anyone to reflect upon the fact that the work he had been doing out here was coming to an end after almost a quarter century. There was nothing remarkable about it. He just strode up onto the porch and into the community hall, walked toward a plain chair at the head of the room, and sat down behind a varnished plywood table, the kind you might pick up at a discount office-supply store. About a dozen people were sitting in chairs arranged casually around the room, and some of them rose from their seats and sat down again. That was the way criminal court began at Alexis Creek, on a sunny morning in late August, Judge Cunliffe Barnett presiding.

Two sheriff's deputies stood at the door, and one of them hushed a group of kids from the Anaham reserve that had been playing noisily on the porch. To Judge Barnett's right, Glen Lucier, the court clerk, was setting out some files on a table of his own. Lucier checked to make sure the tape recorder was running properly, then ran down the names on the daily court list, which consisted of two pages of legal-size paper stapled together. Lucier organized his file folders, one for each case on the list, on the same kind of table the judge was using in place of a dais. Facing Barnett stood Larry McCrea, circuit counsel, and Bill Hilderman, Crown counsel, behind four tables pushed together, arrayed in front of the judge like a kind of makeshift railing, which also served as their desks. At the side of the hall, at another table, sat Lila Gunn from the Native Courtworkers' Office.

The first order of business that morning was the matter of the Crown v. Lee P. Alphonse, police file 201-96-0332, case number 19155-01-00-01. But there was no sign of Lee Alphonse. A sheriff's deputy walked to the door and called out into the parking lot, where small groups of Chilcotin people and Alexis Creek locals were loitering around their pickup trucks, stubbing their boot toes into the gravel and chatting. "Lee Alphonse?" The deputy waited a moment on the porch, turned around, and walked back in. He shook his head. A Native woman told the deputy, loud enough so that Barnett and the lawyers could hear it, that Lee would probably be coming in with Fossie, unless he'd forgotten today's appointment or something. Barnett asked Hilderman if he wanted to stand the matter down for the moment. Yes, your honour, Hilderman answered.

The second order of business was the matter of the Crown v. Louie J. Billy. There were three counts, related to an impaired-driving charge, case numbers 19116-01-00-1 and 19116-02-00-1-C, police file 201-96-267. Louie Billy was not in the room. The sheriff's deputy again walked to the door and called out into the parking lot, where the same small groups of people milled about the same collection of vehicles. "Louie Billy?" The deputy walked back in and again shook his head. "Nope." Barnett shuffled some paper from one file to another. In a barely audible voice, Hilderman told the judge, "He was released, to be here today. He's not here. There should be a warrant." Barnett replied, just as quietly, "Okay."

The same sort of procedure repeated itself in the cases on the list named Sharon Carpenter, Durwin Haines, and Gerald Johnny, and in each case, the proceedings were adjourned. But in the case of Gerald Johnny, Barnett noted that there was nothing in the file to suggest that a summons had been issued. It was not as though Gerald Johnny would have been hard to find. He was the chief of the Anaham Indian Band, the largest of the Chilcotin reserve communities, one of the most populous in British Columbia's Interior. It was only a ten-minute drive away. It was Judge Barnett's last day in Alexis Creek, and here on the court list, of all people, was Gerald Johnny. There was just a hint of what might have been a brief smile on Barnett's face, but not quite a smile. It was more like a subtle furrowing of the eyebrows, a tightening of the lines around his eyes, and maybe his lips twitched just a bit. It was hard to tell what was happening behind the plain glasses he wore. Barnett was sandy-haired, grey-eyed, and gentle-featured, not given to any dramatic expressions.

More files were shuffled from one folder to another on the judge's table, on Lucier's table, and on the pushed-together tables that served as the desks for Crown counsel and defence, until it came time to deal with Nils Kelly, police file 201-96-0412, on a charge of marijuana possession.

Kelly, a B.C. Hydro line-crew driver from Bella Coola, had been found with about an ounce, in two small plastic bags, in his jacket pocket, along with eleven roaches in the ashtray of his 1994 Dodge Dakota pickup truck, which he was driving down the Chilcotin Highway at eighty-eight kilometres an hour in a seventy-kilometre zone when Constable John Clemens of the Alexis Creek RCMP detachment pulled him over. Constable Clemens had concluded, not just from what had come billowing out the driver's side window, that Kelly "appeared to be quite on the stoned side". Kelly pleaded guilty. Barnett told him he wasn't going to give him any stern lectures about the prudence of the country's marijuana laws, but he nonetheless tore several strips off Kelly for driving while he was stoned. "It's just stupid," Barnett said. For his sins, Kelly was sentenced to a $500 fine and three months' probation and was ordered to drive only while on the job. It wasn't a licence suspension, Barnett told Kelly, and there was no cause to involve the superintendent of motor vehicles in the thing. It was a matter of going to the RCMP detachment and turning in his licence, and, in return, Kelly would get a photocopy of his licence, with a copy of the court order under it, and he'd be expected to carry it whenever he was driving a B.C. Hydro truck during working hours.

By this time, Gerald Johnny, chief of the Anaham band, had found his way to the courtroom. Wearing a light-blue shirt, white pants, and brown shoes, he sat in a chair in the community hall, staring at the floor. The charge was public mischief. It involved an allegation that when Johnny called the RCMP to report that his car had been stolen, he was really trying to persuade the RCMP to believe that the reckless driver behind the wheel of his vehicle on the date in question was someone else.

It had been more than twenty years since the first time Gerald Johnny appeared before Judge Barnett. Johnny had played no small part in catapulting Barnett into a strange and dangerous orbit that few provincial court judges in the province's history had travelled. It was an experience that traversed the evolution of aboriginal-rights law in British Columbia and the renegotiation of relations between Native peoples and British Columbia's justice system, and Barnett's part in all of this was concluding, after a fashion, on this sunny day in August. Along the way, there were always newspaper headlines. They began in 1978, in the *Williams Lake Tribune*. One headline raged against "Barnett's leniency". One proposed "Best to Settle Our Own Scores". Another protested "A Typical Form of Justice", and another announced "Meeting Called For on Justice System Problems".

How Gerald Johnny figured into things was that he was the Indian who happened to appear on a charge of car theft, in Barnett's courtroom, back in the days when court day in Alexis Creek was convened in an upstairs storeroom above Pigeon's Store. These were also the days when car thefts in Williams Lake were what some people, without much exaggeration, were calling an epidemic. The culprits were most often identified as Indians, and usually Indians who lived on the Chilcotin reserves of Anaham, just west of Alexis Creek; Stone, just south of Lee's Corners; and Redstone, out on the road to Anahim Lake. Nemiah Chilcotins were rarely blamed for these thefts, mainly because Nemiah was about a two-hour drive down beyond Stone, at the end of a dirt road, on the lee side of the coast mountains. Alexandria was well north of Williams Lake, and if it was necessary to attribute wrongdoing to those Chilcotins, there were enough people up in that neck of the woods who could busy themselves with that. In those days, cars and trucks would disappear from the streets and parking lots of Williams Lake and they'd often be found way out west, in the Chilcotin country, abandoned on a back road, burned and crumpled in a ditch, or upside down in some pasture.

What brought the twenty-year-old Gerald Johnny to stand before Barnett on June 12, 1978, and which produced all those early headlines, was a charge that he was the Indian who stole Truman Henry's pickup truck from a street in Williams Lake on the night of March 20 that year. The Crown's case against Gerald Johnny was that he was the Indian driving the pickup when it was spotted leaving the Dogpatch Inn, where only minutes before, somebody had been breaking into a vehicle in the parking lot, apparently intending to steal a cassette deck. Gerald Johnny was also alleged to have been the Indian standing near Truman Henry's parked pickup truck, flagging down cars and pickups on the Chilcotin Highway near the Meldrum Creek turnoff, asking the occupants of the passing vehicles whether they had any spare chew, which is also known in the Chilcotin as snooze, which is chewing tobacco, a persistently popular commodity in the hills west of Williams Lake. Truman Henry's pickup ended up near Fish Lake. Gerald Johnny was allegedly found there, trying to get it out of a ditch. He was arrested, and several weeks later Johnny found himself standing in front of Cunliffe Barnett in an empty storeroom above Pigeon's Store in Alexis Creek. It wasn't the first time they'd met.

The first time, Johnny was seventeen. The events that brought him before Barnett back then began sometime shortly after 1 a.m., October 25, 1975, on the Chilcotin Highway, just east of Riske Creek. Johnny and his brothers had developed a notorious reputation for themselves in and around the Anaham reserve where they lived, and Johnny had already been convicted of Criminal Code offences. In the middle of the night that October, Johnny and Desmond Hance, an eighteen-year-old Anaham band member, were waiting on the highway at the Farwell Canyon turnoff. They were drunk. It was snowing. Andrew McLeod, a frail, eighty-three-year-old white man, and Elsie Baptiste, an elderly Chilcotin woman, were driving home from Williams Lake, and when their car approached the Farwell Canyon Road turnoff, Gerald Johnny was standing in the middle of the road. He motioned them to stop. Desmond Hance was sitting in his car, with the engine turned off, at the side of the road. McLeod slowed to a stop, and in the following moments, Johnny and Hance pulled McLeod from his car and beat him senseless. Then they went after Elsie Baptiste, and although she was badly beaten, she pulled a knife and managed to stab Hance in the leg, then she fled. Johnny and Hance took off with McLeod's car, leaving the old man on the roadside, and Baptiste managed to get help at the nearby Riske Creek store. McLeod's car was later found, only two miles away, in a roadside ditch. Johnny and Hance were arrested, tried, and convicted, and Judge Barnett sentenced the pair of them to two years in prison on definite sentences, and two years each on indeterminate sentences, and off they went to jail in Kamloops.

They served their time, after appealing and overturning Barnett's indeterminate sentences. Johnny had been out of jail for several months when he was arrested for stealing Truman

Henry's pickup truck in 1978. It was true enough that there was nothing outrageous about the allegation that Gerald Johnny, at Fish Lake, had been apparently in possession of stolen property. The problem was that the Crown's allegations against him weren't supported by any evidence. Nobody saw Gerald Johnny steal a pickup truck. At the Dogpatch Inn, the only witness could offer only that she saw "a truck of some sort", and a month later she fingered Gerald Johnny in a police lineup. As for the requests for chew at the Meldrum Creek turnoff, one witness said she saw "an Indian boy", and the most solid evidence came from a man who said that the young man at the Meldrum Creek turnoff "looked like a Johnny". At his trial, several defence witnesses confirmed Johnny's account of his whereabouts on the day the truck was stolen, and Johnny's story was partially confirmed by a Crown witness to boot. No evidence was entered that it was Johnny who got the pickup truck stuck out by Fish Lake. So Barnett acquitted Gerald Johnny. Nothing in Chilcotin was ever quite the same again.

There were petitions. More than eighty people turned out for a town-hall meeting in Alexis Creek. There were senior representatives of the RCMP, there was somebody there from the attorney general's department, there was talk about putting on "white hoods" and "shooting a son of a bitch" who might be trying to steal pickup trucks. There was talk about clubbing thieves over the head with things. Barnett was there. He suggested that a lot of the crime in Chilcotin was perpetrated upon Native people, and that crime was often as much a function of poverty as anything else, and that crime would likely remain a feature of the Chilcotin country so long as poverty was so extreme. This didn't prompt much discussion. There were furious letters to the editor of the *Williams Lake Tribune*. One came from Irene Bliss, a not inconsequential personality in the Chilcotin, who observed: "It isn't much use taking our troubles to court any more. We had best learn to settle our own scores, until the justice system is improved." Truman Henry wrote his own letter to the Tribune, proposing: "The judge, or the whole judicial system, has to go. Time we all stepped forward to look after our rights."

It fell to Rodney Hawkins, Johnny's defence lawyer, to point out in a letter to the editor of the *Williams Lake Tribune* that the reason some people were angry was because they still held "the old belief that if a native person is charged with an offence he is guilty and any other result is scandalous". All Barnett had to say for himself was that as long as he was a judge in the Chilcotin, it would no longer be good enough to convict a man of a serious crime when all the evidence you could produce was that the culprit was an Indian or that the culprit "looked like a Johnny". That was the way things had been. Those days were gone. By 1978, some people had come to understand that. Some hadn't.

Cunliffe Barnett was appointed Williams Lake's first full-time, legally trained, regular provincial court judge in October 1973. He'd come from a well-to-do Vancouver family, the family that owned Barnett Lumber Industries as well as Forbes Bay Logging, a successful firm with substantial holdings in the Desolation Sound area. He grew up in Kerrisdale during a time when a son who showed some promise was expected to take up something respectable, like engineering. So Barnett went off to the Massachusetts Institute of Technology, in Boston. He graduated as a geologist and a geophysicist, with a second degree in business administration. He worked a year for Imperial Oil in Alberta's Swan Hills. He couldn't stand it. He ended up teaching mathematics and physics at Red Lake, a mining town in northern Ontario whose Indians lived on the margins. He'd married Mary by then, and their first son, Duncan, was an infant. For a while, they lived in a mobile home, then Barnett returned to the coast to work in the family lumber business. He didn't much like that, either. His family wasn't all that happy with all of this.

Around that time, Barnett decided that if people were going to be mad at him for not doing what they wanted him to do, there was no reason not to do what he really wanted to do, which was law. He graduated from the law faculty at the University of B.C. in 1966, articled with Freeman and Company, a big downtown law firm with an office in the Burrard Building, and struck out on his own, opening up a practice in Prince Rupert, in the Besner Block, right across from city hall. He did a thriving business, handling criminal cases in Prince Rupert, Ocean Falls, Masset, and Stewart. After returning to Freeman and Company, and only seven years after he'd been called to the bar, his application to the provincial bench was successful, and he was posted to Williams Lake. He was thirty-seven years old. He and his young family, which now included a second son, Kevin, and daughter Kym, settled down at an old Cariboo homestead. It was a settler's log cabin, out towards Miocene, with no running water. Before Cunliffe Barnett arrived in Williams Lake, the business of judging was done by people like the local hotel manager or the sawmill owner. It was that way all over the Interior. A man would be sworn in as a judge, when necessary, to do mainly whatever the RCMP suggested he should do. That was the way things worked, and when Barnett arrived in Williams Lake, he wasn't exactly warmly received. A significant number of the townsmen weren't sure if they liked the idea of some outsider handling what they considered to be their affairs. As Barnett recalled, the prevailing opinion throughout the Chilcotin and the Cariboo was that the RCMP's job was to keep the Indians in check and to stay away, for the most part, from the affairs of the white community. In some circles, even the idea of criminal trials for Indians was considered rather novel. Criminal and civil matters that involved Indians were regarded as best dispatched expeditiously, without benefit of much decorum or due process, and drawing attention to these cases was bad policy. To their view, the virtue of discretion was proved in its transgression, which is what happened in the case of Fred Quilt.

In the early 1970s, Fred Quilt's name became a household word in Canada. Quilt was a fifty-five-year-old Chilcotin man from the Stone reserve. Depending on whose version of events you believed, he was either a typical drunken Indian who had the misfortune to fall down and injure himself to the point of death while he was being arrested and trundled into an RCMP truck on the Chilcotin Highway, or he was an Indian martyr, an innocent man that a vicious Mountie stomped to death on a Chilcotin backroad. The problem of sorting out the events that caused Quilt's death was not the kind of job that counted for much in the course of administering justice in the Chilcotin country. An inquest was carried out because of the legal requirement to do so. Sid Leith, the local medical-clinic manager, doubled as a justice of the peace and was also coroner. Leith was also a former RCMP officer. He supervised the selection of the coroner's jury, and the Williams Lake detachment of the RCMP made the selections. One of the jurors was an auxiliary RCMP officer. Another juror lived in the same house as two RCMP officers. There were Indian witnesses to the event, but the RCMP interviewed only the white witnesses. No Indian witnesses were called to testify at the inquest. White witnesses were called, and their expenses were paid. And on it went. When the outside world got wind of what was going on, the virtue of discretion was proved. The controversy raged for years.

Barnett was Leith's successor. He got his first glimpse of the way things were handled in Williams Lake during one of the first criminal trials he heard. Barnett had long forgotten the details of the trial itself, but what he remembered about that day was the way the local welfare officer walked into the courtroom, while the trial was underway, and came straight up to the judge and asked when his case would be heard. What case? Barnett asked. The welfare officer told Barnett he shouldn't concern himself with the details, it would only be a matter of issuing a court order approving the apprehension of an infant, and it wouldn't take but a moment because nobody would be there to oppose it. Barnett told the welfare worker to leave and come back later.

At the end of the trial he was hearing, Barnett noticed two people sitting in the back of the courtroom. He asked if there was anything they wanted. They were Mike and Eileen Toby. They happened to be in Williams Lake, a half day's travel from their home in the roadless hills above Chezacut, when they'd heard about the court hearing by accident. Two or three weeks earlier Eileen had given birth to a baby that had been somewhat sickly, and the doctor told the parents not to worry themselves but to leave the child in the hospital in Williams Lake. A welfare officer then went through the routine of announcing a proposed apprehension in the legals column of the classified section of the *Williams Lake Tribune*, and if Mike and Eileen Toby hadn't heard about the proposed apprehension by accident, they would never have seen their child again. It was common practice, Barnett soon learned, and he described it as a practice that was nothing less than the systematic kidnapping of Indian children. In

1976, Barnett paid a visit to Canim Lake, a small Indian reserve of about two hundred people. They asked him if he knew how they could get their children back, or at least find out how they were doing. He was given a list. There were twenty-one names on it. There was nothing extraordinarily complicated about the way they got lost. Indian women would come to Williams Lake to deliver their children in a hospital, the mothers would be told to go home and not worry about their child – he was just a little sickly and needed a few days' care. And that was the last they'd ever see of their babies.

When it came to that kind of institutional cruelty and bureaucratic hard-heartedness, Barnett was fond of saying, as he did during an address to a Williams Lake Kiwanis Club luncheon in 1988 and again to a meeting of the Williams Lake Rotary Club in 1993, that his thoughts often turned to a remark attributed to the American essayist H. L. Mencken: "Every normal man must be tempted, at times, to spit on his hands, raise the black flag, and begin slitting throats." But he was also fond of saying that the alternative had to be more than complicity, and something other than whining about things, and if all you did was sit around and wait for the politicians to catch up to the real world, it would be a very long wait. When it came to questions of Native poverty and child welfare, he wrote to the *Provincial Judges' Journal* in 1989, "Provincial court judges cannot honestly say that we bear no responsibility for creating this situation and cannot contribute to changing it. We are not mere powerless pawns. ... Most of us do not understand the lives and values of aboriginal people. We provide reasons for their common belief that the law often intrudes unfairly to punish people and take children away, and to give circuit judges and lawyers opportunities for sightseeing, fishing, and partying."

Almost twenty years after the eruption over Gerald
Johnny's acquittal on charges of stealing Truman Henry's pickup
truck, on the judge's last day in Alexis Creek, no momentous
event was precipitated by Gerald Johnny's appearance at the
community hall on Anaham's Meadow Road. This was a mischief charge against the thirty-seven-year-old chief of the Anaham Indian Band. The matter was put over for another month.
Johnny took a small red datebook from his pocket, wrote the
court date in it, and got up and walked out of the Alexis Creek
community hall. Then Louie Billy showed up. His trial was put
over until the afternoon.

The next case on the court list was that of Larry J. Sigurdson,
police file 201-95-1007, which involved a charge of driving without due care and attention, which Sigurdson was alleged to have
been doing the day he pulled into the Alexis Creek Mega Fuels
station in his logging truck, bought some candy and pop, fuelled
up, and drove off, ripping out Mega Fuels' pumps in the process,
which caused about $30,000 in damage. It happened just before
lunchtime on a cold November morning, and getting to the pertinent facts and all the details of the incident took more than an
hour of the court's time. It was a bit of a drama.

Sigurdson was acting as his own counsel, so he got to cross-
examine Danny and Wanda Taylor, the young proprietors of
Alexis Creek Mega Fuels. Wanda didn't have all that much to
say about things, and Sigurdson's questions were friendly
enough, but Sigurdson was not particularly happy with Danny
Taylor. Both in their early thirties, Larry Sigurdson and Danny
Taylor had known one another for years and had always been on
friendly terms. Until the incident, anyway. The blond-haired Sigurdson, tall and lanky, wearing a white shirt and a clean pair of
jeans, was clearly displeased with Taylor. Taylor, with a close-

cropped crew cut, sat there at ease in his red work shirt and green pants. Sigurdson was particularly displeased when Taylor told the court, in his description of Sigurdson on the morning in question: "His mental condition I would say was somewhat perhaps less than adequate. I would attribute that to tiredness." This did not help Sigurdson's case much, and Sigurdson probably didn't help himself either when he accounted for his mental state that morning by asking Taylor, who was under oath at the time: "It could be somebody's nature to be inattentive, forgetful – the absentminded-professor syndrome – wouldn't you agree?" Taylor agreed. Sigurdson then put it to Taylor that on the morning in question, rather than having been tired, it was just possible that, being "forgetful by nature", it was every bit as likely that he had been "absentminded or preoccupied". Taylor agreed again.

Taylor had nothing to gain from Sigurdson's conviction. The Insurance Corporation of B.C. had taken care of most of his costs. But Sigurdson was a logging-truck driver, and there were already several motor-vehicle infractions on his record. Over the previous four years there had been an impaired-driving conviction, a number of speeding tickets, a conviction for unsafe passing on the left-hand side of the road, and a dangerous-driving conviction. He clearly could not afford to allow his file to grow much thicker, so he engaged Taylor in a lengthy and fairly professional-sounding cross-examination that touched upon the nature of truck brakes and how they might be affected by slushy snow as opposed to frozen snow. There was close questioning about the precise condition of the ground around Mega Fuels' pumps the morning of the incident, and whether or not large iron pump guards of the type found at the card-lock stations in Williams Lake and 100 Mile House would have helped prevent what had occurred at Mega Fuels.

At one point, after he had been excused from the witness box (which was also a simple chair and a table, like the chair and the table that passed for Barnett's dais), Taylor jumped up from the back of the community hall and shouted to Barnett, "I object, your honour." Barnett explained that things like that happened on television sometimes, but not in the real world. So Taylor sat back down and had to listen, like everybody else, to Sigurdson's explanation about why it would be wrong to find him guilty of driving without due care and attention, and how, in fact, what had happened that morning was simply an unfortunate accident. The proceedings that Taylor objected to involved a large metal object that Sigurdson, rather awkwardly, was asking to have entered into the record as evidence. "What is that?" Barnett asked. "It's a socket," Sigurdson said, explaining that it was a wrench socket, from a socket set that somebody, probably his brother, must have placed carelessly under the seat of the truck shortly before the incident. The socket, Sigurdson explained, had rolled out from under the seat and become lodged under his truck's pivoting gas pedal, causing the truck to accelerate, and while he was madly kicking at the socket, the truck trailer jumped the concrete island at Mega Fuels and carried off the fuel pumps, and that's how the whole thing happened. As to why this explanation was being offered, out of the blue, when it hadn't been offered during his arguments with Taylor after the incident, or, say, when RCMP Constable John Clemens questioned him about the event only minutes after it occurred, and why it was coming out only now, and as a complete surprise to everybody associated with the incident, Sigurdson explained: "I've been through this kind of thing enough times to know that it's best not to say anything. These things can get misconstrued."

Neither Barnett nor Sigurdson had any cause to misconstrue the implications of a conviction, which is how the case con-

cluded. Sigurdson pleaded with the judge, and lamented the life
of a logging-truck driver, how he drives fifteen hours a day, in all
kinds of weather, in snow and cold so extreme that sometimes
the brakes won't work at all, and he drives over rocks and
stumps, and sometimes over cars and other trucks, and "one slip,
you get crucified, because they're out to get you." But the judge
was not swayed, and although the fine was a mere $300, the
judge said he was not unaware of the fact that another conviction on Sigurdson's record would likely result in Sigurdson finding in his mailbox a letter from the superintendent of motor
vehicles letting him know that his driver's licence was suspended.
Sigurdson seemed resigned; at least he took it well. He was dismissed, and as he was getting up from his chair to go, he asked
for his brother's wrench socket back. It was explained to him
that since he had gone to all the trouble of having it entered as
evidence, it would have to be kept by the court for a thirty-day
period, after which he could collect it from the court registry in
Williams Lake. Sigurdson slumped back down into his chair for
a moment. Then he got up slowly and walked out of the Alexis
Creek community hall, into the parking lot and the bright morning sun.

By this time, Durwin Haines had showed up. So had Lee
Alphonse. Their cases were considered briefly, and trial dates
were set, and their business at the Alexis Creek Community Hall
was concluded just in time for the lunch break. Judge Barnett
stood, and so did court clerk Glen Lucier, Crown counsel Bill
Hilderman, circuit counsel Larry McCrea, and Native courtworker Lila Gunn. Barnett strode out of the hall into the parking
lot, and after he'd finished chatting with the lawyers, who had
followed him outside, Lila Gunn took him aside and pulled a
small camera out of her purse. She wanted a photograph of him,

for a keepsake. She'd been a courtworker on Barnett's circuit for eighteen years. She would miss him, she said. Barnett smiled readily as the shutter of the camera opened and closed, and then we made our way down onto what might be described as Alexis Creek's main street, to the Cook Shack, Rudy Thys's little café across from Pigeon's Store.

The lawyers and court staff went to the Chilcotin Hotel restaurant for lunch, but Barnett said there was no way he would step inside that place. As we were walking across the street, Barnett said he hadn't once been inside the Chilcotin Hotel since that incident with Katie. The hotel's food was just fine, he said, and he didn't have anything in particular against the place. The ownership had long since changed hands, anyway. But there was no way he'd go there for lunch, just the same. So it was the Cook Shack, with its paintings of scenes from European towns, and a tabletop with signatures all over it that hung from the back wall as decoration. Lila Gunn joined him at his booth, and shortly after she sat down, Don Brecknock, a local rancher and the area school-bus driver, came over to congratulate Barnett on the occasion of his leaving.

For years, Brecknock had run a successful guide-outfitting business from his ranch, but that all ended when the logging trucks moved in. Brecknock was a justice of the peace himself, and for a while he worked as the manager of the Anaham Indian band office. He asked Barnett about his plans. Barnett replied that he didn't really have any. He was leaving for the coast. That much was sure. He and his wife, Mary, had bought a place in the Gulf Islands fifteen years earlier, but Mary still had a year with the school district to finish up, and they'd be living down on the lakeshore at Williams Lake until Mary's year was over. Barnett kidded about the big truck he'd bought for the move to the islands, and how maybe he'd set up a business and call it Saturna Island Moving and Storage. Or he'd go into another line of work and call it Bigfoot Adventures. He'd bring over German tourists and have them up and down Mount Warburton Pike, on llamas, looking for sasquatch. Whatever happened, he was leaving. His son Duncan was taking over the family place out on Miocene Road, where Barnett had built a spacious log house near the place where the homesteader's original cabin had stood. Duncan had already brought his cattle up from his place in the Hat Creek Valley. At home, everything was in boxes. Barnett and Brecknock chatted some more, and it came time to order. The judge ordered the steak sandwich, rare. Lila ribbed him about keeping away from the hotel, but Barnett said the Cook Shack was just fine by him. More than ten years had passed since that whole thing with Katie. Barnett said it was the principle of the thing. He left it at that.

There had been four counts against Katie Ross. It was alleged that on or about the 31st day of August 1985, Katie attempted to murder Joe Denby by stabbing him with a knife. That was one count. The others were assault with a knife, aggravated assault with a knife, and possession of a dangerous weapon (a knife). Barnett's ruling in the case caused an uproar, but as he wrote in his judgment, when he acquitted Katie Ross, "it is not the judge's job to try to make people happy by deciding cases in certain ways." His written decision in the Katie Ross case left a lot of people, in places like Alexis Creek and Williams Lake and Anahim Lake, a lot less than happy. His point was that a confrontation between an intoxicated Native woman and a white businessman, in which the businessman gets stabbed, does not, of necessity, involve criminal wrongdoing by the Native woman. It wasn't like the judge said Joe Denby got what he deserved, or anything like that. But it was close.

> In the circumstances of this case, it is necessary to make some comments concerning the character of Denby. He and a partner, Al Dixon, operate the Chilcotin Hotel at Alexis Creek. The hotel contains a beer parlour, and many of the patrons of the establishment are Native people, whom Denby obviously scorns. He keeps a club behind the bar and has used it to inflict harm upon unruly Native persons. He keeps a mixture of cleaning ammonia and tabasco sauce behind the bar and has sprayed that into the eyes of unruly Native persons. I am satisfied that he has a well-deserved reputation for unreasonable violence among and toward members of the Alexis Creek Native community and that Katie Ross was aware of this on August 31, 1985.

Katie Ross was a fifty-three-year-old Chilcotin woman who had come to town that day with her kids, in the family pickup truck, to join in Alexis Creek's Pioneer Days celebrations. Katie got drunk, and she went to the Chilcotin Hotel that afternoon to drink some more. The hotel contained the only beer parlour for hundreds of miles in any direction. Katie was removed from the beer parlour, so she got mad. Outside the hotel, on the street, she was shouting and throwing boards at the hotel. The sensible thing would have been to ignore her until she went away, or to call the police. The Alexis Creek RCMP detachment was a mere three hundred yards from the Chilcotin Hotel. Instead, Joe Denby came out and started throwing boards back at Katie and engaged her in a shouting match. Katie's sons gathered up the boards she and Denby were throwing at each other to keep them out of Katie's reach, but Denby, unsatisfied, started hurling beer bottles at her. Katie's sons managed to drag her away to the family pickup truck, which was parked across the road, over by Pigeon's Store.

Denby followed. He later claimed that Katie threw a five gallon garbage pail at him, but Barnett doubted that part of his story. At any rate, Denby chased Katie onto the porch of Pigeon's Store and pushed her across the porch, where she fell on the ground. Katie's son Roland then tackled Denby, saying, "You can't do that to my mother," or words to that effect, but he wasn't exactly sober, and at first, at least, he was no match for Denby. The next thing, Roland and Denby fell through the store's front door and were rolling around on the floor inside, and Roland soon had the upper hand. By this time, Katie had picked herself up, dusted herself off, and in through the doors she went.

She had a pocket knife on her person. In my experience, every Chilcotin Indian woman does. Such knives have many uses in the Chilcotin. Sometimes, unfortunately, they are used in ways that cause injuries to other persons. Sometimes that use is offensive, on other occasions the use is defensive.

Katie stabbed Denby twice. Then she walked out of the store.

Not surprisingly, Katie's actions ended Denby's activities that day.

Katie's decision was "most unwise", Barnett found, but that wasn't the issue. A reasonable fifty-three-year-old Chilcotin woman might well have concluded that the brawl underway between Roland and Denby on the floor of Pigeon's Store was simply an interlude in what was, in Barnett's view, "an outrageous assault upon Katie Ross". Barnett conceded that a danger in his decision in the case of Regina v. Katie Ross was that some people who didn't like his way of administering justice would be sure to call his finding "a license by the judge to go around carrying a knife and producing it". So to be sure there would be no confusion, he noted that it wasn't about anything of the kind. It was just that the Crown had failed to prove that Katie Ross had been acting in a criminally wrongful way, and the mere fact that a Native woman had stabbed a white man proved nothing. So Barnett thanked Crown counsel for his thorough presentation of the evidence against Katie, then he thanked Crown counsel for all the case law that had been cited for him to help him come to a decision, and then he dismissed all charges against Katie.

And that's where the Katie Ross story would have ended, except for what happened three years later.

The death of Katie Ross gained the same kind of notoriety that Fred Quilt's death produced almost twenty years before, but in Katie's case, a coroner's jury produced the remarkable recommendation that the colour of a person's skin should not be a factor in determining whether or not to call an ambulance for a sick person. The jury found that just such had been the case in a decision that had to be made about how to get Katie Ross from the Red Cross outpost in Alexis Creek to the hospital in Williams Lake, almost two hours east. It was at that outpost that Katie ended up, on a warm June evening in 1988, writhing in agony for reasons nobody at the clinic could determine.

There had been a shoot-out that day. Dennis Jack, a troubled young man from the Redstone reserve, had gone berserk and set out on a rampage across the countryside. Years earlier, Dennis had been sent to prison for getting drunk and shooting Terry

Hunlin in the chest at point-blank range. Hunlin died. After Dennis got out of jail, he came back to the Chilcotin, got drunk at the Anahim Lake Rodeo, returned to Redstone, where he had been staying since his release, and stole a pickup truck. He had a .22-calibre rifle with him. Dennis was carrying the rifle when he came across Katie and her husband, Peter, at their cattle camp at Bidwell Meadow. He shot and killed Peter. There were other shots. He ended up leading police on a seventy-three-day manhunt throughout the Chilcotin, which ended for him in a hole he had dug for himself underneath a house at Redstone, with RCMP sharpshooters surrounding the house and a helicopter hovering in the sky. He killed himself by shooting a bullet into his head.

On the night of the day Dennis shot and killed Peter Ross, with Katie not all that familiar with the English language and complaining about terrible pains in her stomach, the staff at the Red Cross outpost at Alexis Creek decided against calling an ambulance for her and left it up to Katie's sons, Roland, Harry, and Albert, to find a pickup truck, find some gas, and get Katie into Williams Lake on their own. Which they did. More than fifteen hours after she was admitted to the emergency ward of Cariboo Memorial Hospital, Katie died, restrained to a cot the hospital staff called a "posey". All that time, nobody noticed the bullet wound in Katie's back.

There were a lot of hard questions at the inquest. It came during a time when the forced and tenuous peace that had been hammered together between the Chilcotin people and the culture that had colonized them seemed to be coming apart at every nail. Ages-old intelligence was being lost to the people as sure as blood from an unbandaged wound. People were dying.

The older people noticed how people died, and they'd point out from time to time that in the Chilcotin, you couldn't just change the way things had always been done without there being some consequences. For many things, if something wasn't done just the right way, death could result. There was a man who came home to Stone after too many years away, and there was no one left to describe the necessary precision involved in casting a spell to make a woman love him, and the spell was badly cast. Night after night, the woman wandered in circles out in the fields, around and around, until she died.

The younger people noticed how people died. Up at Kluskus, Chief Roger Jimmy said that when he looked to the southwest, he could tally the number of Indians who would die a violent death that year by adding up the miles of new logging roads into the country. While B.C.'s logging industry grew from a harvest of thirty million cubic metres of timber in 1961 to ninety million cubic metres in 1989, the volume of timber leaving the Chilcotin in the 1980s alone quadrupled. The Williams Lake sawmills were working round-the-clock shifts, and the old Chilcotin economy, a mix of cattle ranching and guide-outfitting, fishing and hunting, was falling to pieces. More than two hundred fully loaded logging trucks were rumbling out of the Chilcotin country into Williams Lake every day, roaring past Indian reserves where eight out of ten adults were on welfare. The young chiefs put together a few impressive-looking logging-road blockades, but the fact was, as Redstone Chief Larry Guichon put it, the Indians were dying along with the countryside. He had no qualms about saying that nobody out there cared, because when an Indian died, it was just an Indian.

Grace Anne Haines was just an Indian. She was raped and thrown to her death from the Sheep Creek Bridge in 1979, and her assailant was sentenced to five years on a manslaughter charge. Ita Elkins was just an Indian. She was beaten to death by her white husband on the streets of Williams Lake in 1982, and several passersby who were called as witnesses at his trial said they did nothing because there was nothing unusual about such a sight. Fred Quilt's brother Eddie was murdered in 1984 when somebody threw him off a cliff. Nobody bothered reporting it. In Alexis Creek, RCMP Staff Sergeant Dennis Alexander said he was as frustrated as anybody else, but the fact was that a crime would be committed out in Chilcotin and nobody would come forward and report it to the police. He said it all seemed to have something to do with the history of the country, but whatever it was, things tended to get complicated when Chilcotin people found themselves involved, in any way, with the law. Williams Lake County Court Judge Howard Hamilton caused no end of consternation in the attorney general's office in Victoria after he threw up his hands in court one day and wondered loudly and publicly whether the Chilcotin Indians would end up just killing one another off unless they started finding reasons to believe in the justice system.

In the weeks after Katie's death, a car loaded with kids from the Anaham reserve flew off a cliff on the steep hill that winds down into Hanceville. An Indian boy who saw it ran down to Bill Spill's store at Lee's Corners, and Spill called the RCMP right away. The next day, the same Indian boy walked back into the store and asked Spill why dead people from the car wreck were still hanging up in the trees. Deanna Marie Harry was fourteen. Daphne Rose Harry was fifteen. There was Marril Sam, twenty-four, Norman Edward Stump, twenty-four, Victorine Dick, twenty-six, and Jacintha Sam, twenty-seven. At thirty, John Bill Sam was the oldest. He was still alive, but barely. He'd been up there all that time. It turned out that an RCMP search began, and a search-and-rescue team headed out on the highway after the call came in the day before, but nobody could see anything anywhere, no matter how hard they looked, so they gave up and left it at that.

The Indians were dying along with the countryside, just as Larry Guichon said. A Stone woman and an Oblate priest who set out on an informal mortality study, done in pencil on sheets of foolscap paper, listed the causes. Their list showed thirty-eight deaths among the 250-member Stone band over a thirty-four-year period, and only twelve of those deaths could have been called natural. The rest were shown as stabbed, shot, alcohol, dysentery, fire, and so on. John Baptiste was an old man who starved to death in cattle camp when his relations got so drunk they forgot they'd left him there. Marvin Haller was another old man. He froze to death after being thrown out of a bar in Williams Lake. Samson Dave suffocated in the back of a pickup truck on the way back from Williams Lake because the others with him passed out drunk in a heap, on top of him. At Toosey, home to one hundred Chilcotins, forty-three people died over a forty-four-year period, and only thirteen deaths could be called natural. The rest: car accident, fire, shot, drowned, and so on. At Redstone, home to two hundred Chilcotins, there were sixty-three deaths over the same period, and, again, only thirteen were natural. The rest were listed as suicide, knifed, burned to death, murdered, and so on. One of those on the list was Terry Hunlin, who was killed by Dennis Jack, who got out of jail, came home drunk from the Anahim Lake Rodeo one day, beat up the woman he was living with, stole a green 1976 Ford pickup, and headed east to Bidwell Meadow, where he killed Peter Ross and fired the bullet that lodged in Katie's stomach and that nobody noticed all those hours before she died.

To Chilcotin Indians, and to many people among the Chilcotin's settler population, Katie and her husband, Peter, were persons of great dignity and presence. The day Katie and Peter were buried together up at Chezacut, more than four hundred people showed up to say goodbye.

But to some people around Alexis Creek, Katie had a different kind of reputation. To be fair to Heather Bailey, the nurse at the Alexis Creek Red Cross station the night Katie was brought in, the issue wasn't quite as simple as the colour of Katie's skin. Apart from whatever mistakes Bailey might have made that night, Katie didn't speak much English, and she wasn't exactly coherent. The gunshot wound was remarkably small. But the thing was that whatever Heather Bailey knew about Katie, it was from the stories she had heard. Katie could get violent, or so people said, and the choice that night was either to call in an ambulance for the long ride to Williams Lake, or just have her sons look after it. Bailey chose the latter. After all, Katie was the one who stabbed Joe Denby that time after her son Roland tackled him and pinned him on the floorboards at Pigeon's Store.

Those were the things that added up to enough of a reason, to Barnett's way of thinking, to take his lunch, on his last day at Alexis Creek, at the Cook Shack instead of the Chilcotin Hotel. The steak sandwich was fine. Lila Gunn and I had cheeseburgers. They were fine too. As we were leaving, Lila pointed out a small Polaroid snapshot pinned to a notice board on the wall, just inside the restaurant's front door. It depicted the carnage at the Mega Fuels pumps next door, taken on the November morning just after Larry Sigurdson had stopped by to take on some diesel. There's the evidence, Judge, she said. So it is, he said, and smiled.

By the time we got back to the community hall on Anaham's Meadow Road, a small group of Nemiah people was assembled in the parking lot. Rena Lulua was there, along with several members of her family, and Joyce Quilt was there. It had been a long time since I'd seen them. I'd lived out at Nemiah for a few months, years before, so we said our hellos and we agreed that we were all thankful for the breeze that had finally picked up and was smoothing the hard edges around the afternoon sun. Rena was quiet, but there was time enough for some small talk among the rest of us. The important questions concerned the health of Henry Solomon, who was still going strong but getting on in years, and how Gilbert Solomon was faring since he'd sworn off the practice of living inside a house. He was camped out in the bush behind the old rodeo grounds someplace, and people didn't see him around much, but he seemed perfectly happy about his arrangements. It was heartening to hear news about Gilbert. We used to stay up late, singing "I'm So Lonesome I Could Cry" and "My Pocket's Got a Hole In It" in Chilcotin. Gilbert's brothers would arrive, one by one, until it was four o'clock in the morning, and there were fiddles and melancholy harmonies that were not always thoroughly discordant. So it was good to hear about Gilbert, and then there was the Stone rodeo coming up that weekend. The big excitement was the mountain race and who'd be up to it, and who'd miss the whole thing because they'd be off to that big wedding over in Deadman's Creek. But the gossip had to end because the judge was already back at his table inside the community hall, and Rena's case was coming up.

It was one of those cases that would never result in one side winning and the other side losing. It was about three-year-old Calvin Lulua. His father was Malcolm Stewart Miller, the short young man with deeply set blue eyes who arrived at the Alexis

Creek community hall that day in a white shirt and a pink tie that was a bit too long, so he'd tucked the end of it into the front of his jeans. He came with his mother and a brother, all the way from Prince George. He wanted to say that the Lulua household, and the Nemiah Valley, was not a fit place to raise Calvin. He sat at the table beside McCrea and fumed during more than an hour's worth of other people's testimony to the effect that, in fact, he was much less fit as a parent for Calvin than Rena Lulua, who sat expressionless, but obviously a bit timid about everything, beside her lawyer, Jeff Huberman.

Malcolm and Rena had struck up a relationship in the Nemiah Valley, where Malcolm had been staying. He'd had some odd jobs, and one of them was working in a salmonid-enhancement project on Chilko Lake. It was clear that he didn't feel much at home around Nemiah, and it was just as clear that Rena felt more than a little bit out of place in Nanaimo, where the pair were living through most of Rena's pregnancy. They moved back to Nemiah, and Malcolm managed to find short-term work now and again, but it meant he was away for weeks at a time. Whatever it was that brought them together, it wasn't strong enough to last very long, and by Calvin's second birthday, there wasn't much left to keep his parents together. Things went from bad to worse after Malcolm had a nasty showdown with Rena's father. Malcolm was ordered to clear off, but he wasn't much inclined, so the whole thing was pretty tense. Rena was asking for permanent custody of Calvin and an order denying Malcolm any access to the boy. Malcolm said that, for the moment, he was asking only for custody of Calvin for a week out of each month, but that later he'd be applying for full and permanent custody on the grounds that Nemiah was a bad place for Calvin because the people out there went on drinking binges, they were always out hunting or fishing, or haying, or moving their cattle around their far-flung meadows way up in the mountains. Malcolm said that although Rena might have testified that she wasn't a drinker, he had once seen her drink from a bottle of beer outside a dance, and for all he knew, her family was "feeding Calvin alcohol" already.

Constable John Clemens was called as a witness for Rena's side. The year before, there had been calls to the Alexis Creek RCMP office reporting that Malcolm had gone haywire out at Nemiah and was uttering death threats and generally behaving in a mad fashion. Clemens headed out to Nemiah one early October morning to find Malcolm sleeping, apparently, inside a black van outside the Nemiah Valley Indian Band offices down on Xeni Lake. Clemens knocked on the van and called on Malcolm to wake up, but he didn't move. So Clemens banged on the side of the van, and banged and banged. Still Malcolm didn't move. By Clemens's reckoning, this meant that Malcolm was refusing to respond to him and was refusing to come out of his van as he was ordered, so Clemens broke a door open. Malcolm still refused to move. Finally, Clemens got frustrated and shot a squirt of pepper spray inside the van. Malcolm stirred and reached for something that Clemens thought might just be a gun, so Clemens pulled his service revolver and pointed it at Malcolm, ordering him at gunpoint to get out of the van (what Malcolm reached for turned out to be bear repellent, which is a little less offensive than a gun, but a bit nastier than police-issue pepper spray). In his defence, Malcolm described the whole scene as one in which he was asleep one moment, and the next "I was abruptly awoken by Constable Clemens, who was pepper-spraying me."

Whatever happened, Clemens handcuffed Malcolm and sat

him in the back of the RCMP van and headed back out of the valley, but it was only a few minutes into the long and dusty drive back to Alexis Creek, with Malcolm carrying on about how Clemens should just stop the van and shoot him to put an end to all his miseries, when Clemens turned around to find Malcolm had managed to draw his handcuffed hands from his back, around under his feet, and he was hanging out a window. Clemens slowed down a bit, but the van was still moving along at a pretty fair clip when Malcolm jumped out, got up, and ran off into the woods. This precipitated a ground search with tracking dogs, and an air search from helicopters. Clemens put the word around to the few people in the Nemiah Valley that Malcolm might still have counted as his friends that he should just be sensible and turn himself in, which he did. He went to court and got saddled with a probation order that obliged him to stay at least a hundred kilometres from Nemiah, but he frequently violated the order, and a few months after his escapade as an at-loose fugitive, Malcolm was arrested again, in a vehicle on its way out of the Nemiah Valley, after an incident involving a smashed stove and broken windows and doors being kicked in. Rena said the whole thing was causing her to fear for her own life, and Calvin's life as well. From Rena's side, there were several stories about Malcolm swinging axes and smashing things up and that kind of thing, and what it all boiled down to, Rena said, was that she was afraid for Calvin's safety and she didn't want Malcolm having anything to do with him.

Barnett carefully considered the evidence. He took notes throughout the whole testimony, every now and then admonishing McCrea and Huberman when they were laying things on a bit thick. When it came time for his judgment, he recounted the pertinent events and summarized each side's arguments. He noted the comments of Malcolm's mother, who testified on her son's behalf and said of Rena: "To be honest, I think she's a fine person. She works hard. She's caring. I know it's hard raising a family, that's for sure." So what it came down to was whether Malcolm Stewart Miller, who'd just finished a brief jail term for violating a court order and was still on parole, should have some access to his three-year-old son, whom he obviously loved dearly. And it came down to whether or not to agree with Rena Lulua, a young Nemiah woman with a full-time job as a secretary at the local band office, at $1,400 a month, that Malcolm should be denied any access to her three-year-old son.

"I think the picture that emerges is, in some ways, pretty clear," the judge said. His finding was that unless and until Malcolm could show some stability in his life, he could not see Calvin. And even if Malcolm proved to be the world's best father, a week out of every month of Calvin's young life, spent in a faraway place with a man who was probably almost a stranger to him by then, probably wasn't a very good idea. As for Calvin's custody, he ordered that it be granted solely to Rena, and before Malcolm could see his son again he would have to prove to a family counsellor that his life had settled down. Barnett asked whether Rena would give Calvin presents, say, if Malcolm sent some along. She said she would. He asked her whether she'd read letters to him, if Malcolm wanted to write some. She said she would. And that was that.

There were some last matters to attend to. A sheriff's deputy had brought Terry Squinas into the community hall, in handcuffs. Squinas was alleged to have been driving while prohibited on the day he was found sitting behind the wheel of a car the RCMP came across in a ditch, but Squinas said it was his sister who was driving, and he was just trying to get the car out of the ditch. He hadn't shown up for a previous court appearance on the charge, and he'd been picked up and sent to jail for eighteen days for failing to appear. His sister Betty was nowhere to be seen. Barnett dismissed the original charge. It was two years old. Squinas was uncuffed and released.

The last item of business involved one of the Isnardy boys. He'd been pinched for using a stolen credit card, and there was an assault charge and a court-ordered curfew that he'd broken and some hours of community work that he'd refused to do. There was no sense in packing him off to jail to wait for trial. He lived with his dad, who was none too pleased with the boy's behaviour. The matter was put over to September. After that, the deputy announced "Order in court", then "Court is adjourned for the day."

Lila Gunn wanted another photograph of the judge, so he took time for that. There were handshakes with the Crown lawyer and the defence lawyers, and some laughs, and then it was over. There were a handful of court days yet to go, elsewhere, and then it would all be behind him. Barnett gathered up his few papers, said goodbye to the sheriff's deputies, and strode out of the community hall in the same casual way he had walked in that morning.

For all the plain old human suffering that had passed in front of him all those years, it was not without the occasional triumph. Much could result from even the most dreary and routine cases.

There was the case of Laura Norberg, a Native woman who worked in a local sawmill, whom Barnett had convicted on a narcotics charge in 1985. Laura had been obtaining prescriptions for painkillers without letting on that she was getting other painkillers on another prescription. She had broken the law. Some judges would have left it at that, but Barnett noted in Laura's pre-sentence report that she had become addicted after she'd suffered a bad job of dental surgery, and a local doctor, instead of finding treatment for her, had been feeding her habit in return for sex. Dr. Morris Wynrib ended up charged with trafficking in narcotics, but the Crown stayed the charges on humanitarian grounds – he was old and had cancer. With Barnett's help, Laura sued the doctor, but the B.C. Court of Appeal wasn't so sympathetic with her. The high-court judges relied on a nineteenth-century case, involving a servant girl and her syphilitic master, to rule that Laura Norberg was no better than her doctor and deserved none of their help.

It was only the year before that Barnett had written in the *Provincial Judges' Journal* that judges were "not mere powerless pawns" in addressing questions of social justice, so in 1990, after the B.C. Court of Appeal rendered its decision in Laura Norberg's case, Barnett wrote about the case in the quarterly magazine of the B.C. Trial Lawyers' Association. He called the decision "an insult to every woman in Canada". You could say some heads turned. Norberg's case became national news. Some judges started a petition to have Barnett reprimanded. Barnett stuck with Laura Norberg. When she was busy helping the lawyers prepare her case, Barnett minded her kids. She appealed the decision to the Supreme Court of Canada. She won.

In 1978, the year he dismissed Gerald Johnny on the charge that he stole Truman Henry's pickup truck, Barnett sentenced a troubled youth in the coastal Native community of Bella Bella, a young hell-raiser named Frank Brown, to a traditional sentence: banishment. Brown was forced to spend several weeks alone on an isolated island, where he was provided with basic food and shelter and was visited only occasionally. Years later, Barnett was invited back to Bella Bella and was the honoured guest at a potlatch Brown sponsored. The boy had gone on to become an artist, a carver, and a canoe-builder.

It was also in 1978 that Barnett dismissed charges against a Chilcotin man named Francis Haines, who had been arrested for shooting a moose out of season. There were some aboriginal rights involved in this, Barnett reckoned. The provincial government appealed Barnett's ruling, and a county court judge said Barnett was wrong, and the county court judge offered a lot of nonsense about how some Chilcotins had freezers and pickup trucks, and Francis Haines was sent back to Barnett for sentencing. Barnett refused and sent the file back to the county court judge with a note: "You convicted him. You sentence him."

Throughout the 1980s, federal fisheries managers were still routinely and quite casually ordering Indians away from their fishing stations on the Fraser River and the Chilcotin River without lawful justification. Just as routinely, the Indians would sneak back to their fishing stations. They'd get arrested and they'd come before Barnett, who quite routinely dismissed the charges against them. In one case, Barnett compared the federal government's purported justification for its fisheries-management decisions to "the kind of propaganda you'd expect from some Eastern European country".

On April 3, 1985, William Alphonse, a Shuswap man from the Sugarcane reserve just south of Williams Lake, shot and killed a mule deer during the closed season, on private land. This wasn't just hunting on Crown land. It was an assertion of aboriginal rights on private land, namely, land owned by the Onward Cattle Company Ltd., about seven miles south of Sugarcane.

Alphonse appeared before Barnett at the courthouse in

Williams Lake. The trial lasted thirteen days. When it was over, Barnett ruled that there was no legitimate conservation concern present, and it didn't make any difference that it was the closed season, or that William Alphonse didn't have a hunting licence, or that it was private land. Barnett ruled that William Alphonse was exercising his rights according to Shuswap custom, and those rights had never been extinguished, no matter what some politicians said. The federal government had never extinguished Indian hunting rights. The provincial government wasn't competent to extinguish Indian hunting rights. Because Section 35 of the Constitution had recognized and affirmed aboriginal rights since 1982, no government had the authority to extinguish aboriginal rights. And that was all there was to it.

The provincial government appealed Barnett's ruling to county court. A county court judge overturned Barnett's decision, but Alphonse had a lawyer, and his lawyer appealed the county court ruling. The B.C. Court of Appeal heard the case and released its decision along with seven other major aboriginal-rights cases, all at once. Those cases included the Vander Peet case, which involved aboriginal fishing rights, and the Delgamuukw case, the landmark Gitksan-Wet'suwet'en aboriginal-title trial that B.C.'s Chief Justice Alan McEachern himself had ruled on two years earlier. McEachern was, after a manner of speaking, the appeal court judges' boss. But his aboriginal-rights findings in Delgamuukw were, for the most part, thrown out. In some of the eight cases, you could say the Indians won. In others, you could say they lost. Among the eight decisions, the Alphonse case was one of only two cases that all five appeals court judges agreed upon. There were no dissenting opinions. They all upheld Barnett's findings and confirmed William Alphonse's rights, entirely. Most of the other cases ended up appealed to the

Supreme Court of Canada. The Alphonse decision was never appealed, and remained, on that last day in Alexis Creek, the last word on aboriginal hunting rights in British Columbia.

But as the years were passing, Barnett was finding that a growing number of trials he had to preside over seemed just plain stupid and worth nothing of any value to anybody, one way or the other. That was what he had to say, more or less, in the case of Regina v. Verlyn Bateham, Sr., In The Provincial Court of British Columbia Held At Queen Charlotte City, Reasons For Judgment of the Honourable Judge C. C. Barnett, August 24, 1995.

Bernard Caffaro served as Crown counsel in the Bateham case. After Barnett was through with him, Caffaro probably wished he hadn't been involved in the thing in any way at all.

Verlyn Bateham lives on 320 backwoods acres in the Queen Charlotte Islands. In 1993 Mr. Bateham bought a few pigs: They were to be a school project for his son and also the family expected them to earn their keep by rooting out and clearing brush.

A fenced enclosure was built. But Mr. Bateham was not wise to the ways of pigs. They were soon escaping and wandering off to enjoy the delights of freedom on a regular basis. Their favourite place was a small meadow near the seashore, a small subdivision, and the highway.

The pigs rooted around in the meadow. That bothered Conservation Officer Smith, who thought he was witnessing the destruction of wildlife habitat.

The presence of the pigs concerned the mothers of some children living in the subdivision.

Fisheries officer Sjolund testified that the pigs did not damage any fish habitat.

In the fall of 1993 Mr. Dawson was driving on the highway one night. A pig was on the highway. Mr. Dawson did not see it. His vehicle hit and killed the pig. The repairs to Mr. Dawson's vehicle cost about $300.

Some local residents got the notion that it was okay to hunt the pigs. Conservation Officer Smith knew this was happening.

Conservation Officer Smith spoke to Mr. Bateham in October 1993.

Mr. Bateham told him the pigs were domesticated European wild boars and that he would try harder to keep them confined.

Conservation Officer Smith also talked to the wife of Kevin Rae. She told him that her husband had told her that Mr. Bateham had told him he was intending to establish stocks of feral pigs so that they could be hunted for sport. On May 20, 1994, Conservation Officer Smith talked to Kevin Rae, who repeated this silly story. Conservation Officer Smith did not question Rae intensely: If he had done that, he might have learned that Rae was one of the "sportsmen" who had stolen a pig from Mr. Bateham and put pork in his freezer.

Later in the day on May 20, 1994, Conservation Officer Smith went looking for the pigs. He was accompanied by Const. Erichsen. The two officers went to Mr. Bateham's home, and when they did not find him home, they had his son show them the pig enclosure which was admittedly in a state of disrepair then. The pigs were not there.

The pigs were found in the meadow. The officers shot six pigs. One pig escaped. The carcasses were delivered to Mr. Bateham and Conservation Officer Smith told him that a report would be made to Crown counsel who might decide to press charges.

And thus it was that Mr. Bateham came to be charged under the Livestock Act: It is alleged that he wrongfully allowed swine to be at large.

The trial of this charge consumed the entire court day of July 17 and most of the day of July 21. One wonders why the attorney general thought that this trial was necessary.

Mr. Bateham believes that his pigs were sometimes assisted to escape by "sportsmen" such as Kevin Rae. I expect that did sometimes happen. But the evidence does establish that in May, 1994, Mr. Bateham was making no real effort to confine the pigs and that he knew they were considered to be something of a nuisance by some reasonable persons.

The charge is proved. But nevertheless, I feel compelled to say that this prosecution was an unnecessary, silly, and absurdly expensive exercise which touched upon the borders of persecution.

You could say that it was the kind of trial that was enough to tempt a normal man to spit on his hands, raise the black flag, and begin slitting throats. It was also the kind of thing that gave Barnett reason to want to pack it in. Circuit duty was interesting, but it meant being away from home and family for days on end sometimes, year after year, travelling on sunny days and on snowy days. Besides, it was probably good for the law to have judges retire early. There was nothing worse, Barnett said, than a crotchety old judge.

In Chilcotin country, some things had changed for the worse in the twenty-three years since Barnett arrived, but there were some things that could be said to have changed for the better. A lot of public attention had been attracted by the Katie Ross inquest, the logging-road blockades, and the kids who died in the trees on the hill coming down into Hanceville. In 1992, B.C. Attorney General Colin Gabelmann appointed Judge Tony

Sarich to serve as a commissioner, under the Inquiries Act, to look into the problems. Barnett would never admit to it, but it could not be denied that he and his judgments played no small part in the decision to set up the Sarich inquiry. More than once, Barnett had publicly recommended just such an investigation.

Wherever Sarich went, he encountered the Chilcotin view of what Alexis Creek RCMP Staff Sergeant Dennis Alexander had said, about how a lot of the problems seemed to have something to do with the history of the country. In the history of the Chilcotin country, the first contact between the British legal system and the Chilcotin people took place with the arrest of six Chilcotin leaders in 1864, following the events that had come to be called the Chilcotin War. The war had its causes in a white man's threat to bring smallpox upon the Chilcotins and in the mistreatment of Chilcotin women in Alfred Waddington's road-building camps in the Homathko Canyon. When the Chilcotin leaders were arrested, nineteen white men and three Indians had died in the fighting. The first judge the Chilcotins encountered was Judge Matthew Baillie Begbie, whose approach to the trial of the Chilcotin leaders was that the blood of white men "calls for retribution". Even in 1864, among the white people of the Colony of British Columbia, public opinion was divided about the appropriateness of arresting the Chilcotin leaders. They had come down from the hills, as evidence in their trials made plain, expecting to negotiate peace. They were hanged. What happened way back then remained unresolved in the minds of the Chilcotin people, Sarich commented, and he observed that the Chilcotin people seemed to have very long memories. Among the 179 "incidents" reported in Appendix D of the Sarich report, Incident Number 096 was reported in the following synopsis: "Elderly woman escorted through court building in handcuffs and terrified because of lack of comprehension of process and irrational fear of hanging."

Barnett appeared before the Sarich inquiry in Williams Lake. In his submission, Barnett said:

> I believe when a Chilcotin person appears before a court in 1993, the judge encounters the ghost of Begbie J. He bent the rules to permit the judicial execution of men who were not criminals. It is very difficult for a Chilcotin person to have faith in our justice system.

Sarich spent months investigating incident after incident after incident. He conducted hearings in several communities throughout the Cariboo and Chilcotin country, and he heard story after story, grievance after grievance. Much discussion centred on the impact of residential schools, particularly St. Joseph's Mission north of Williams Lake. The hearings were underway at a time in British Columbia's history when hundreds of Native people were coming forward with evidence that was resulting in assault, rape, and buggery convictions against priests and ministers, church officials and school officials, even the bishop of the Williams Lake diocese, Hubert O'Connor.

Sarich made a host of recommendations. He said that in the absence of a treaty, the province should enter into an accord with the Chilcotin leadership about the conservation of forest resources. He suggested that the provincial government establish at least one alcohol treatment centre in the Cariboo-Chilcotin. He said trained interpreters should be available during trials of Chilcotin, Shuswap, and Carrier people who don't understand enough English to know what is going on, and, wherever possible, trials of Native people should be conducted in their own communities. He said a Native police force should be established to work with the RCMP, and Native peacekeepers should be trained for small communities like Nazko, Nemiah, and Kluskus. Native communities should become more involved in sentencing decisions, Sarich said. The RCMP was urged to improve its public-complaints process. Sarich also recommended that the provincial government issue posthumous pardons to the Chilcotin leaders of 1864 who Begbie had convicted and hanged, and that their graves be located and marked by a suitable memorial.

The provincial government accepted many of the commission's recommendations. The government did not issue a pardon for the hanged Chilcotin chiefs.

The night of Cunliffe Barnett's last day in Alexis Creek, we were talking about his early days and what it was that made things turn out the way they did, when the subject turned to what was going to come next. We were out in a pasture, and the moon was full, and the night was so bright we could see Duncan's Herefords on the other side of the lake.

Barnett remembered travelling through the Deep South during his college days when he first glimpsed what life was like for black people there. And then there was Mary's father. The man was a building contractor, in Virginia, and after a particularly hot day, he'd bring home some of his black employees so they could go for a swim in his pool. His neighbours despised him for it. When Barnett was teaching at Red Lake, Ontario, he had noticed how things were not all that different with Indians in Canada. It struck him that Indians had been invisible in his childhood, and even though he and Cole Harris, a childhood friend, used to hunt tadpoles down on the Fraser River by the Musqueam reserve in Vancouver, he didn't learn until he was an adult that there was a reserve there and that Indians lived on it. He knew there were Indian women around Cowichan who knitted Indian sweaters, and he knew Indians on the Queen Char-lotte Islands had carved totem poles, and he remembered from his boyhood summers on Savary Island that Indian women would row their little boats over from the reserve on Harwood Island, and his mother bought fish from them. But that was all he knew, and he couldn't quite understand why. As for what he was going to do with his life now, he started in again about Bigfoot Adventures, and German tourists on llamas, and Saturna Island Moving and Storage. It was hard not to wonder if he'd been passing off this same story to some of the Williams Lake towns-men, putting the word out that these were his plans, precisely. Once, he had a court clerk alter a lawyer's copy of a trial tran-script, changing the lawyer's words to read: "Don't listen to what the Court of Appeal says. They're just a bunch of old fools." He could still laugh about that.

"I don't know," he said. "You know, the hostility I used to hear expressed so openly about Indians, in the Chilcotin country, I haven't heard that in a while."

There was a long silence as he gathered his thoughts. Barnett was known for those silences. He'd stop in the middle of a sen-tence sometimes, look at the ground, scratch his chin, stare into space, then start up again, sometimes minutes later, where he'd left off.

"But I do not know, by any means, that I have the best feel for that kind of thing, or how real the changes are. Or how deep the changes are."

In the few weeks before his last day at Alexis Creek, Bar-nett had been making headlines again in the *Williams Lake Tri-bune*. The headlines included this one: "Judge Barnett Declines

Meeting with City Council on Auto-Theft". As had been the case back in the 1970s, car thefts in Williams Lake were again becoming what some people, without much exaggeration, were describing as epidemic. The townsmen were unhappy with the situation. Indians were fingered as the most likely culprits, and lenient judges were seen to be contributing to the problem. Williams Lake city council was busying itself, in council meeting after council meeting, with the "massive problem" of car thefts, and the problem of sexual offenders released from prison into the community, and the problems of a politically correct federal government with all its liberty-infringing gun-control laws. A local "court watch" group had been set up in Williams Lake to monitor judges' decisions. In a letter to Barnett, Williams Lake Mayor Walt Cobb said that, in future, city council would expect that in every case of a second or third conviction on car-theft charges, the maximum sentence of ten years should be imposed, and juvenile car thieves should be raised to adult court on their first offence, and if they weren't raised to adult court for some reason, then the maximum sentence of two years should be imposed in each case. And if Cunliffe wanted to say anything about these things he could appear before town council, the local "court watch" group, and the local community police group.

In a letter to Williams Lake councillor Charlie Wyse, Barnett expressed the hope that "when elected community leaders choose to criticize, they would first make some attempt to know what they are talking about". He continued: "Judges cannot be beholden to politicians at any level. ... The courts in Canada are, and must appear to be, impartial. They cannot be subject to political interference and influence. These principles are fundamental and elementary but apparently not well understood within council chambers in the city of Williams Lake."

If Barnett seemed a bit testy about these things, it might have been because he was in the middle of a case called Regina v. Arthur Long.

Arthur Long was an upstanding citizen of Williams Lake, a forty-year resident, a supervisor with one of the local forest companies, an auxiliary RCMP officer, and firearms instructor. A true townsman. He was "the hard-working, ever-obliging guy next door", Barnett wrote. After fourteen years of marriage, Long decided to have an affair. When his wife complained about it, he choked her. When she complained again, he grabbed her, twisted her arm, dragged her outside, and threw her into the snow. When she complained about it a third time, he smashed her head against the refrigerator, held her down on a bed, choked her, and threatened to kill her. Like too many women in that sort of situation, Arthur Long's wife stayed, and stayed silent. On the night of June 9, 1995, Arthur Long beat his wife, and he continued beating her for several hours. He tied a rope around her neck. He put a knife to her throat and tore off her shirt and told her he was going to cut her up into little pieces. Finally, he smashed her face into the floor, had a shower, went to bed, got up the next morning, and went off to the loggers sports day. His wife finally went for help. When the police searched Arthur Long's house, they seized seventy-five firearms. The weapons included an unregistered handgun, a sawed-off rifle, two loaded rifles in a bedroom closet, and a "crude but effective" silencer.

Long was charged on seven counts. He pleaded guilty but asked for a sentence of four months, which wouldn't threaten his job security. The Crown lawyers wanted Long put away for four years. Barnett sentenced him to eighteen months in prison, followed by two years' probation, and he ordered that Long not go anywhere near his wife and that he be prohibited from possessing any kind of firearm for ten years. Barnett also made what he called a suggestion. A technicality prevented him from ordering it, so it was just a suggestion, and it was that Arthur Long sell his weapons collection and donate the proceeds to Chiwid House, a women's transition facility that had opened not long before in Williams Lake. He mentioned once that, at the time, he considered recommending that the guns themselves be turned over to the women at Chiwid House, but he allowed that some people might think that would be going a bit too far.

In the opening words of his written reasons in the case, Barnett had this to say:

This case should be a terrible jolt to some leading and many good citizens in Williams Lake.

There are leaders in this city who believe that the theft of pickup trucks is the central criminal problem in Williams Lake. They also believe that this problem would somehow go away if judges would do their duty and impose vengeful sentences.

Although they are usually careful not to say it, these community leaders also believe that the good people of this nice little family-oriented city are in no way responsible for the crimes that happen here. That is because they believe that the criminals really come from the Anaham Indian Reserve about 100 kilometres west of Williams Lake.

These beliefs were all made known to me when I arrived here as a new judge more than 20 years ago. Some of them were repeated in a letter which the mayor sent me a couple of weeks ago.

But life is not so simple.

Back in the house, everything was in boxes. Mary was going to bed, and the moon was rising in a clear black sky over the rolling Cariboo hills.

Spring had stayed late, and it had been a rainy summer, so all over the country, the hay fields and alfalfa fields were scattered with round bales and square bales, and a second crop was coming up all around them. It was a beautiful night. It had been a beautiful day. Other than that, there had been nothing remarkable about it.

Where the Noxnox Sits

It is a vast and barren plain of jumbled and broken volcanic rock, the kind of landscape that might belong on some distant planet, except there is a slippery mud road through the middle of it and a line of telephone poles stretches off into the distance and disappears into the horizon. The road went on and on in this way, through sleet and rain, until it became possible, between the swipes of wiper blades across a muddy windshield, to make out an intersection in the distance. At the crossroads, a sign pointed to the north.

Welcome to the Home of the Four Crests. Gitwinksihlkw. People of the Lizard.

Gitwinksihlkw is a small Nisga'a village nestled against the north wall of the valley. At the highest point in the village stands the Bear's Den Pole. At the top of the pole, a long-beaked bird-like creature keeps watch over the houses below. It is the Supernatural Being that played such an important part in the events that caused the landscape to be formed this way, and its eyes gaze out across what could have been the bottom of Death Valley or somewhere in the middle of Australia, except there was wet snow half-covering everything and there were distant blue-green mountains appearing now and then from behind clouds.

Immediately beneath the Supernatural Being is a wolf, then a hunter holding a bow, then a bear, which is a crest of the wolf clan, and the bear's seven ribs protruding. Then there is a circle, which is the bear's den. Then there are lizards on each side of the pole, and below them, a large human figure. Two humans, arms interlocked, stand above another large human figure, representing a chief. There are human faces, representing the Gitwinksihlkw families of the four Nisga'a clans – the wolves, the eagles, the killer whales, and the ravens – and then a large human figure again, holding another human figure in his arms.

At the base of the pole stood Dennis Nyce, the compactly built, thirty-six-year-old Nisga'a eagle-clan member and carver whose apprenticeship began with his work on the Bear's Den Pole. Alver Tait was the master carver. Dennis's cousin, George Gosnell Jr., worked on it too. They started it in 1990, and it was raised in 1992, to stand in front of the new community hall. It was the first pole erected in Gitwinksihlkw since the preposterous pole-wrecking mayhem that fanatical Christianity ushered into the Nisga'a country around the turn of the century.

Dennis had spent the morning helping his wife's uncle, Alvin Azak, get his boat ready for the trip down to his father-in-law's camp at Fishery Bay for the annual oolichan run. And then, in the early afternoon, he was standing at the base of the pole, shivering in a light shirt, trying to explain the meaning of the

images on the pole and the heraldry and the sagas they are intended to represent, and how all of these things were connected somehow to the events that had placed the Nisga'a people at the centre
of another upheaval, this time over a document called the "Nisga'a agreement-in-principle". The document was intended to
provide the basis for the first treaty concluded west of the Rockies since 1871, when British Columbia entered Confederation.

The controversy was electrified with allegations of secret government covenants and the quiet establishment of laws that seg-
regate Canadians according to their ethnicity. In the *Prince
Rupert Daily News*, commercial fisherman Dana Doerkson was
predicting that the federal government would soon step in and
confiscate non-aboriginal fishing boats in a repeat of World War
II measures against Japanese Canadians. He also predicted, face-
tiously, that local NDP MLA Dan Miller would defend the construction of a local prison, for dissident fishermen, on the
grounds that it would be good for construction workers and provide permanent employment for prison guards. In Terrace, at
Caledonia High School, someone scrawled "Whites Against
Native Rights" on a wall in the boy's washroom, the most recent
little eruption there in a series of incidents that had been underway for several years. In Vancouver, the Fisheries Council of B.C.
– the lobby group for the coast's biggest fishing companies –
declared that the coast-wide fishing industry had been betrayed
and would be destroyed as a result of the Nisga'a deal. Throughout the province, logging companies and cattlemen were joining
with the fishing companies, pitching in $25,000 for full-page
advertisements in the Vancouver dailies complaining that they
hadn't been consulted properly about the Nisga'a agreement. In
Ottawa, Reform party MP Jim Abbott complained that the deal
was racist because it wouldn't allow him to become a Nisga'a

chief, while his colleague, Reform MP Keith Martin, blasted the Nisga'a agreement as "apartheid" and called on the federal and provincial governments to scrap the whole thing. Martin routinely bought his own advertisements in Victoria's newspapers. In one, Martin set out his legislative agenda on aboriginal issues, and in a mere five hundred words he managed to find room for the terms "law and order", "armed thugs", "attempted murder", "commercial fisheries based on ethnicity", "double standard", "preferential treatment", "smuggling of drugs, weapons and alcohol", "criminal acts", "criminal activities", and "anarchy".

But it was raining hard, and a cold wind was blowing on the hill overlooking Gitwinksihlkw, and Dennis's nephew, Isaiah, was waiting in the car. Down in the village, in the warmth of his house, Dennis's kids – Kyle, thirteen, Kerrie, eight, and Errol, seven – were watching Sunday-morning cartoons, and Dennis's wife, Natalie, was on the phone to a cousin, asking whether the oolichans were showing up yet down at Fishery Bay. So it was enough to say that this pole, with the long-beaked Supernatural Being at the top, was raised in the memory of Louisa Oyea, who was Dennis's father's great-grandmother. She was a beautiful woman. Her father turned down so many of her suitors that she eloped with a white man, Billy Moore, and travelled with him to Victoria. Her father, a high-ranking killer-whale chief, led an expedition to Victoria to plead with his daughter to return. He found her there, and she agreed to come home and quietly slipped away with her father's party. Moore followed them, and the story may have come to an unhappy end had it not been for the canoe that Louisa's father deliberately capsized and left behind, which fooled Moore into believing that his wife had drowned, and caused him to give up the chase.

As for the Supernatural Being and the part it played in the convulsions that produced a landscape so eerie and so unlike anything associated with British Columbia's coast, there is a story to account for that. There are boys tormenting fish, a violation of a cardinal tenet of the ayuukhl – the ancient laws that govern the Nisga'a people – which admonishes against any sort of disrespect for animals. The boys stick tiny pitch lamps in the backs of salmon, just to watch the lights swim away in the river. The animals take their vengeance and bring a great fire against the land and the people. A supernatural bird intervenes. Its beak holds back the flow of lava down the valley, saving the downriver villages from their certain destruction.

In another story that accounts for the creation of this same landscape, it was a volcano that erupted at precisely that moment in history when white people are known to have first ventured in ships in the vicinity of Chatham Sound, more than a hundred kilometres to the west. It was the Spanish ship *Sonora*, with Lieutenant Juan Francisco de Bodega y Quadra in command. In August 1775, at 55 degrees and 17 minutes north, Quadra's crew "suffered from the heat", according to the priest aboard the ship, "which they attributed to the great flames which issued from four or five mouths of a volcano and at night-time lit up the whole district, rendering everything visible".

In any event, several hundred people were buried in the molten rock, or so the story goes, and the peculiar desert of the Upper Nass Valley was formed. Before these events, there was a pool on the north side of the valley that was inhabited by strange lizards. There was a village there, Gitwinksihlkw, which is properly translated as People of the Place of the Lizards, and the pool became a bend in the Nass River, which was forced around the lava flow to run a new course below the mountain wall on the valley's north flank. Gitwinksihlkw was once accessible only by trail through the mountains or by river canoe. By the early 1900s, there was a road into the valley, and it was a short shunt across the river in punts, or a walk across the ice in winter. In the 1960s, the footbridge went in, a swaying, cable-hung suspension bridge across a canyon, and from then on the village came to be known as Canyon City, and that is how I remember first entering the place, years earlier, to visit Harry Nyce at his salmon net at the bend in the river, where we watched the seals bob and weave in the current, all that distance from saltwater. In 1995, after years of petitions, a road bridge was built across the river. Gitwinksihlkw's own Jason Gillis, twenty-one, one of the bridge crew, died of heat exhaustion on the job one day. Since the bridge went in, when the road up from Terrace is passable you can drive right in to Gitwinksihlkw, population 250.

As for the new community hall, it was built to replace the one that burned down the night old Percy Azak died. It was built through the efforts of people like eighty-six-year-old Peter Nyce, who begged pledges for a walkathon, and nobody reckoned he'd be able to walk more than a block. He walked five miles and raised hundreds of dollars, so people from all over the valley forked over their pledge money, amazed. In one night, the people of the Nass Valley raised $150,000 for the hall in a telethon.

Nearby is the village of New Aiyansh. Farther down the Nass River there is Laxgalt'sap, and finally Gingolx, on the seacoast. Gitwinksihlkw is the smallest Nisga'a village, and it is as healthy looking as reserve communities get. Every village resident is a shareholder in a village logging company, and the company owns a small sawmill, and there is a salmon-enhancement project and other jobs here and there, and the unemployment rate, for much of the year, rarely rises above fifteen percent. About

2,500 Nisga'a people lived in the valley, and about 3,000 Nisga'a lived elsewhere, mainly in Terrace, Prince Rupert, or Vancouver. About three hundred non-Native people lived in the valley, mainly at the logging camp, Nass Camp.

We got back in the car and drove down the hill, toward the new elementary school, to look at another pole. We talked about the agreement-in-principle. Its main points were easy enough to discern.

About one tenth of the Nisga'a territory would be in the hands of the Nisga'a, who would govern themselves by laws consistent with the laws of Canada and British Columbia. Outside that core territory, the Nisga'a would retain some secure access to mountain goats, moose, timber, and other resources to be shared with people from outside the territory. A provincial court would be established in the Nass Valley, and $200 million would be set aside to assist the Nisga'a in the transition from being wards of the Indian Act to being a self-governing community, with village governments and a range of infrastructure components not unlike those of a regional district. There were provisions governing public safety, public works, traffic and transportation, schools, and other matters no different than what any non-aboriginal community would expect as a matter of course in modern society.

In the most controversial element of the deal, the Nisga'a would be allowed to partly restore their economic relationship with the rich salmon resources of the Nass River, independent of the Prince Rupert fishing companies. Widely reported as a guaranteed share of twenty-eight percent of the Nass River salmon in a "Nisga'a-only commercial fishery", the agreement actually proposed the Nisga'a be granted a small fraction of the salmon catch they enjoyed before the canneries came. About $11 million would be set aside to allow the Nisga'a to purchase fish boats. The Nisga'a would be guaranteed the equivalent of about 120,000 sockeye when the runs were healthy – far fewer fish, on a per-capita basis, than many smaller Native communities were already harvesting all over the coast, in the absence of any treaty rights. In a side agreement, the Nisga'a would be guaranteed the chance to catch more, and to sell them if they chose, according to a formula that guaranteed the coastal commercial fishing industry the lion's share of the Nass River's harvestable salmon surplus. The deal also denied the Nisga'a the opportunity to establish their own major fish plants for at least twelve years after the signing of a treaty, another concession to B.C.'s fish processors. In some years, the Nisga'a allocation could reach twenty-eight percent, but that was only twenty-eight percent of whatever was left over after spawning-escapement goals were met, and after the Alaskan fleet took its share (which often amounts to about half of all returning Nass River salmon, landed in Alaskan ports where some of the same B.C. fishing companies that were campaigning against the Nisga'a agreement had established fish plants), and after "incidental harvests" from other B.C. fisheries were also deducted.

The agreement-in-principle was overwhelmingly ratified by the Nisga'a after a four-day assembly in the valley, but there were many Nisga'a who had their own serious doubts about it all. It was criticized in the valley as the product of negotiation by exhaustion, a deal concluded by aging Nisga'a chiefs who had pointed out more than once that they had grown old in the negotiations, which began in 1973. These same chiefs had expressed concern about the prospect of a change in the party in power in Victoria, and what that change might mean for a treaty concluded later. There were Nisga'a people in Gingolx who said their village was shortchanged, with most of its important territories excluded from the core territory. There were Nisga'a people in Vancouver who protested that they were not adequately consulted.

Dennis Nyce was a nephew of Hleek, whose English name is Joseph Gosnell Sr., who had served as the chief Nisga'a negotiator since the July 1988 death of his brother, James Gosnell. James Gosnell was the tireless crusader for treaties in British Columbia whose imprint on the national imagination was his famous declaration at the 1985 constitutional talks that B.C.'s Native people owned the province "lock, stock and barrel".

Dennis had worries of his own about the agreement the Nisga'a chiefs had signed. He said he could not understand how the Nisga'a could remain within their own law, the ayuukhl, and still agree to hive off lands and call them Nisga'a lands but at the same time exclude lands outside the core territory. He said he did not know how the landscape – which was always clearly and precisely defined in the ayuukhl and appears as an elaborate patchwork of distinct territories, each associated with an individual simo'ogit, a hereditary chief – could be carved up in such a way, with some territories no longer owned by the Nisga'a or the simo'ogits, and other territories owned by the Nisga'a people but not the simo'ogits.

"It does bother a lot of people," he said. "In a sense, the government pulled the same wool over our eyes the same as they did when they first introduced these things to our people. But when I look at that map in the [agreement-in-principle], I see this as an admission of guilt. That's why they gave some of those lands back. By giving this back, they are saying, 'A mistake was made.'

My uncle says we have to make compromises. He's right. We know darn well, the political and economic way things are headed now, if we reject this, next time maybe what we'll get will be smaller. So we made compromises. We had to."

The agreement-in-principle was 178 pages long. One fifth of the document catalogued "cultural artifacts" removed from the valley over the previous century or so that were held by the Canadian Museum of Civilization and the Royal British Columbia Museum. The artifacts were intended to be repatriated. Each artifact was carefully identified. There were soul catchers, charms, masks, rattles, whistles, clubs, axes, pipes, spindle whorls, grindstones, neck rings, blankets, carved figures, spoons, looms, bracelets, boxes, and feast bowls. There were no provisions in the agreement regarding the estimated 68 million grams of gold, 2 billion grams of silver, 13.6 million kilograms of zinc, or 389 million kilograms of copper removed from the valley by the mining industry over the years. There was no mention of the millions of board feet of timber taken out of the Nass Valley since the 1940s. There was nothing to compensate for the two hundred square kilometres of clearcuts in the mountain forests around Meziadin Lake. There was no mention of the churches, and no mention of residential schools.

We drove past Gitwinksihlkw's new Salvation Army citadel. It is a place that does not attract many people anymore, Dennis said, just some old people who kept their faith in that church, and some of their grandchildren. For Dennis, it was a difficult thing to discuss. Ten years before, in the middle of the night, he stood with a knife in his hand, in his darkened house, and he wondered why he was standing there, and why it was that he intended to kill his family and then himself. But somehow he knew he had a choice. He knew he could cross over, or at least put it off. So he put the knife away. The next day, he talked to his brother, Steven. It was about what had happened to him, beginning at the age of six, at the village schoolhouse. He had never told anyone before. It had gone on for years. Salvation Army minister William Gareth Douglas would take Dennis into a small room and sexually abuse him. Steven encouraged Dennis to talk to the RCMP. And then Steven had said, "Make sure to tell the RCMP that the same thing happened to me too." What Dennis Nyce set in motion resulted in seventeen grown men from Gitwinksihlkw coming forward, and in April 1988, William Gareth Douglas was sentenced to nine years in jail. But Douglas was not the only nightmare that haunted Dennis's sleep. Dennis also spent some of his childhood far away from Gitwinksihlkw, at the St. George's Indian residential school in Lytton. The dormitory supervisor there routinely took children from their beds in the middle of the night and molested them. A few days after Douglas was sentenced in a Prince Rupert courtroom, St. George's dormitory supervisor Derek Clarke, in a Lytton courtroom, was sentenced to twelve years in prison on several counts of buggery and indecent assault. In passing sentence, Judge Bill Blair said that by a "conservative estimate", Clarke was guilty of at least 140 sexual assaults on children.

At Gitwinksihlkw's new school stood the second pole raised in the village in modern times, carved by Alver Tait, Art Nyce, Vernon Azak, Richard Morgan, Robert Tait, Dennis Nyce, and others. At its top, Txeemsim, God's messenger, appears as Raven and holds onto the sun. Holding onto Txeemsim's leg is a being in transformation, part human, part animal. Then there is a lizard, then a killer-whale fin, then a raven, then a large human figure who holds her daughter with two small hands. There are two children below them, then a lizard, then a wolf, an eagle, then two boys carrying a big salmon, then a simo'ogit who is holding his nephew.

It's a long story. It slowly unfolded at the kitchen table at Dennis's house, where the kitchen and living-room walls were decorated with pictures of his children and the children of his relatives. Dennis was talking about the oolichan fishery and Easter, both approaching, both events bound up in redemption and salvation, both as certain as the words Blood and Fire, which appear above ornately stylized Nisga'a u-forms and ovoids painted on the old, crumbling Salvation Army church that still stood in Gitwinksihlkw. There is Blood and Fire, Oolichan and Easter, God the Father and Kam Ligi Hahlhaahl, the Chief of Heaven. There is God the Son and Txeemsim, the Raven, the messenger of the Chief of Heaven and the one who brought order to the North Coast. There is God the Holy Spirit, the Noxnox, the spirits that have always been here, along with the ayuukhl, which had codified what Christians understand as the commandments and the doctrine of forgiveness of sins long before Captain George Vancouver sailed into Observatory Inlet in 1793 and became the first white man to be greeted by the Nisga'a.

Long before the volcano, and long before the churches came, there was the ayuukhl, which Dennis Nyce credited with saving his life and the life of his family. There is nothing in the ayuukhl that could provide for such a thing as murder and suicide. And Dennis had not lost his faith, and in spite of everything the church had taken from him, it could not take that away from him. The day the agreement-in-principle was signed, it was coming up to Easter, the long winter over, the oolichans coming home, and although something had died in all of this, something else was being born. Blood and Fire. Dennis Nyce had known both.

"There are two roads in life," he said, setting out a thing the old people in Gitwinksihlkw say. "Red and black. They run parallel. The black road starts smooth. Gets treacherous. The red road is good. Everything you want, you'll get. You've always got a choice. You can cross over. They say when you hear the hissing, burning, and crackling in a fire, those are the sounds of the unfortunate ones who didn't go the right road."

And then he was quiet for a moment.

"I consider myself blessed," he said. He nodded his head toward Natalie, Kyle, Errol, and Kerrie. "This was my road to recovery. They were."

It was a hard road. He grew up in a family of five brothers and three sisters, and his parents were people who worked hard to keep their children fed and clothed and had little choice but to send them away for schooling. His father, Jacob Nyce, was a fisherman, the president of the Native Brotherhood of B.C. Among the few happy memories Dennis had kept from his childhood were the moments when his imagination was captured by the masks in the basement of his family's house, and the vague memory of being stood up at a feast when he was a boy, and given the name Naxk-kwsdins, from his mother's family.

There was a way to understand the agreement-in-principle, Dennis said. It was difficult, but it was a way to understand the whole strange history of it. In that history, there was a delegation of Nisga'a chiefs that travelled to Victoria in 1860, when the town was the colonial capital. The chiefs went to Victoria to ask how it could be that the Queen owned their land, and they were turned away. There was 1872, the year after B.C. was admitted as a province of Canada, when B.C.'s Indians were denied the vote and remained barred from voting for almost a century.

There were the potlatch laws of the 1880s, which banned the institutions that were at the heart of First Nations government, culture, and economy, and which also made it illegal to dance without the permission of the superintendent-general of Indian Affairs, and all those laws stayed in force until 1951. There was the federal law that made it illegal to bring the question of aboriginal title before the courts, or to raise money or hire a lawyer to press a land claim, and that law effectively kept British Columbia's unresolved land question a secret from 1927 until 1951. There was the Supreme Court of Canada's 1973 decision in the Calder case, named after the Nisga'a leader Frank Calder, which split narrowly on the question of whether aboriginal title still prevailed over British Columbia, and which caused the federal government to begin the process of negotiating the settlement of comprehensive claims. Then there was the B.C. government's 1990 decision, during Bill Vander Zalm's term as premier, to join Ottawa in negotiations with the Nisga'a.

One way of understanding this history, Dennis said, begins with Txeemsim. It is Txeemsim who appears as a raven at the top of the pole that stands in front of Gitwinksihlkw's new school. Txeemsim travelled to heaven during that time in human history when people and animals were not distinct from one another. He travelled with his brother Wiigyet, who is like Txeemsim and also conventionally appears in the form of a raven but who is better known to the Gitksan people, the southern neighbours of the Nisga'a.

Txeemsim was told by a village prophet that during his voyage to the sky he would encounter a great mountain, and a mountain pass would be blocked by a great obstacle in the form of a sheer, smooth-faced rock wall. Regularly, at intervals, the wall would open and close. Four times a day it would open, and each time it would quickly close again. The obstacle was called Mismaa. Txeemsim was warned to observe it closely and note very carefully the time it took to open and close.

After studying Mismaa carefully, Txeemsim and Wiigyet finally outwitted it and passed through to the garden of the Chief of Heaven, Kam Ligi Hahlhaahl. They bathed in a pool, where they were discovered by Kam Ligi Hahlhaahl's two daughters, again just as the old seer in Txeemsim's village had foretold. The two young women had come to gather water, and they saw two beautiful birds. One sister said, "Let's catch them and bring them home," and she and her sister wrapped Txeemsim and Wiigyet in human clothing and carried them back to the house of the Chief of Heaven. There, the two brothers revealed that they were humans, from the earth, and the daughters were afraid for what their father might do. The brothers guessed that they would be killed.

But Kam Ligi Hahlhaahl had heard his daughters talking, and they sounded happy. He guessed that he had visitors, and he wondered how they had passed through Mismaa. He confronted the two men, and questioned them, and was impressed that they had passed through the barriers he had placed against intruders. Kam Ligi Hahlhaahl then granted his daughters to Txeemsim and Wiigyet as wives, and after some time had passed, his daughters gave birth, and their children fell to earth. One child landed at the mouth of the Skeena, in a kelp bed. The other landed in the Nass Valley, near Txeemsim's house. The Skeena child was found by a Metlakatla seal hunter and was adopted by a Skeena chief who had lost a son. At Txeemsim's village, the baby had fallen to earth at the village cremation ground, where a chief's wife, who was also mourning the loss of a child, heard a baby crying and went out and found the child, and rejoiced.

And this is what it has been like, with the struggle over aboriginal rights and title, with this history since the volcano, and with this desperate struggle to survive as a distinct people, finally signing an agreement-in-principle and hoping it would survive and result in a treaty a year or two away, Dennis said.

"This is not make-believe," he said. "These are events that actually took place. So for us, this AIP and everything we've done, it has been like this great obstacle, and the people had to learn how to pass through it. We came face to face with Mismaa. And we have overcome it."

The new bridge at Gitwinksihlkw has a pole at each of its four corners, representing each of the four Nisga'a clans. The southwest pole is a raven, the southeast pole is an eagle, the northwest pole is a killer whale, and the northeast pole is a wolf. The wolf pole was the first pole Dennis Nyce carved on his own. It depicts a wolf atop a noxnox and a bear. The name of the pole is Where the Noxnox Sits. The pole has its origins in a December 1989 community gathering, where Dennis vowed to follow the vocation of a dancer and a carver, and he further promised to carve a pole for his father and his father's clan. Alver Tait helped him design it, but Dennis did the rest, from the selection of the log to its debarking, and from the hollowing of its core – taking the back out – to the arduous and delicate work of carving. Where the Noxnox Sits is carved in the classic Nisga'a style, not engraved, the way Gitksan and Haida carvers are inclined to carve, but truly sculpted, shaped with deeply pronounced features. It is sparse and understated and starkly beautiful.

Dennis spent the days leading up to Easter down at Fishery Bay, at his father-in-law's fish camp. They were bringing in the oolichans, busy with the hard work of making grease, that strange concoction rendered from the oil of the fish that had

come to mean life redeemed and prayers answered for so many
Native communities of this coast. Dennis had never made grease
before, and he said it was all new and wonderful. He got back to
Gitwinksihlkw for Easter dinner and for some time with Natalie
and their children and other relatives visiting from away. And
then it was back down to Fishery Bay for a few more days, and
then home again, and back to his plans to build the first Nisga'a
canoe from Gitwinksihlkw since his grandfather's time. He was
thinking about more poles, and he wanted to encourage a revival
of the practice of raising mortuary poles, long since abandoned
in favour of headstones. He wanted to see a pole carved for Jason
Gillis, who died building the bridge. He said he wanted to see all
kinds of poles, all over the village. He figured that before his own
life was over, he'd carve twenty or thirty more poles.

Oolichans

In the wheelhouse of the *Escorial II*, making the short jog up the slough from his houseboat to the main stem at New Westminster, Mark Petrunia let on that as far as he was concerned, the sea lions knew what was going on, and the seals probably knew too. Rounding the upriver tip of Annacis Island, where the Fraser River divides to become the Main Arm and the North Arm, Petrunia also let on that to his way of thinking, it might be that the seals and the sea lions had become wretched in their wisdom, lurking in the river the way they were, lying in wait for him to tear at his nets.

"They know what I'm doing," he said, just as a seal surfaced about three boat lengths off the port side of his gillnet boat. "They know what's going on."

What was going on that afternoon was that Mark Petrunia was headed for the same spot in the river he had been visiting in his gillnet boat every day since the oolichans arrived a month earlier, accompanied as they always are by clouds of seagulls. Petrunia's daily routine, shared by two other gillnetters – Harold Wolf downriver and Jimmy Adams up at Katzie – involved a fifteen-minute set, on the backup tides, to maintain an exact record of catch for analysts with the Department of Fisheries and Oceans. He was also gathering samples to be sent on to the Pacific Biological Station in Nanaimo, where people in lab coats would analyze oolichan DNA, fish scales, age, sex, milt, and eggs so humans might know a little, at least, about whatever it was that the seals and the sea lions knew.

After what had happened that year, there was nobody at the Department of Fisheries and Oceans or the Pacific Biological Station who would lay claim to knowing what had caused the strange and disturbing events that were taking place up and down North America's West Coast involving populations of Osmeridae, the extended family of smelts that includes the oolichan. All anybody knew was that oolichan populations were suddenly disappearing from rivers where they normally spawned predictably and in the hundreds of millions. They were appearing in rivers where they had never been known to spawn. Massive herds of Pacific white-sided dolphins were showing up in inlets where they had never been seen before, and they were feasting on oolichans. Autumn-spawning capelin appeared to have vanished from the waters south of Alaska, and just when their extirpation was about to be pronounced a certainty, an unknown population was found up the fjords of B.C.'s Central Coast, up Wakeman, Knight, and Kingcome inlets – spawning in the springtime. Longfin smelt, also saltwater fall spawners, were showing up in the spring, far up the Fraser River, ready to spawn. And in the midst of all the confusion, the Fraser gillnetters who set their nets for oolichan were finding themselves surrounded by herds of harbour seals, California sea lions, and those giant, 10-foot brutes known sometimes as northern sea lions and sometimes as Steller sea lions, the old bulls weighing as much as a ton. The herds would move in and rip the fish from the mesh and tear the nets to shreds.

When these bizarre events began to unfold, fisheries scientists were at a loss to make any sense of it because so little was known about the Osmeridae. That's because none of the half-dozen or so species that occur on the B.C. coast were in any way important to the commercial fishing industry, and it's the industry's priorities that determine research effort. There was a time when oolichans were an important commercial fish, but the processors who set up fish-oil plants on the Nass River in 1877 soon found that the Nisga'a ate so much themselves that there weren't enough fish left to render down to oil for export. Around the turn of the century, the fishing companies moved in on the Nass again, and a thriving industry producing fresh, salted, and smoked fish kept oolichan in fifth place among the coast's fisheries until 1912, when competition from other smelt fisheries around the world pushed oolichans out of the world market. In the late twentieth century, the only commercial oolichan fishery on the coast had been a small gillnet fleet of a dozen or so boats on the Fraser. Apart from these few gillnet boats, oolichans remained important only to Native communities, and mainly for that peculiar, lardlike product known as oolichan grease, that most precious of aboriginal trade commodities, rendered from tubs of boiled oolichans that have been first left to rot for as long as three weeks.

It can take up to twelve tons of rotting oolichans to produce a mere two hundred gallons of grease, and the practice of grease-making is conducted according to rigid rules, some of which are serious enough that you're expected to potlatch away the shame if you violate one of them, and each set of rules is as unique and distinct as the languages of the peoples who carry on the grease-making tradition – the Kwagewlths, Haisla, Nuxalk, Heiltsuk, Tsimshian, and Nisga'a. Local custom determines the choice of fish, whether or not a male oolichan is propped up on the "stinkbox" to oversee the process "to ensure fair play", what the ratio of male fish to female should be, whether or not to line the planked stinkboxes with cedar boughs, whether at a particular rivermouth a human hand may come into contact with rotting oolichan, how long to let the fish rot, how long to boil the mash, and whether to strain or not to strain and how thoroughly. Old Andy Siwallace at Bella Coola insisted that grease must be cooked twice by no other method than red-hot rocks taken from a fire or the taste would be ruined, and the whole thing would be shot any-way unless it's scooped up at precisely the right time, when the sound of the boiling grease reaches just the right "tune".

Oolichan grease provided a rich and necessary dietary supple-ment with all sorts of reputed curative powers, but it was also a condiment to liven up a steady winter diet of dried salmon and dried berry cakes and dried deer meat. It was the unlikely cur-rency of precolonial trading empires and the main item of trans-port along elaborate networks of trading trails known as grease trails that extended from the coast far into the Interior. These were the trails followed by Alexander Mackenzie in 1793, when he earned the distinction of being the first white man to traverse this continent north of Mexico. He finally came upon the Pacific Ocean when he stumbled out of the bush near Bella Coola.

Oolichan grease is valued and rated according to individual taste and preference, the way different kinds of wine are valued in European culture. There are entire villages on this coast that

maintain they can discern from the colour or the consistency or
the flavour or the smell whether a particular serving of grease has
come from the Kitlope or the Kildala or the Nass, and some old-
timers will say they can narrow it down to the family that made
it. Varieties of grease are at least as numerous as the variant
spellings applied to the Chinook-jargon word for the fish, which
include oolichan, eulachon, hoolakan, hoolikan, oloachen, olla-
chan, oulachon, oulacon, ulchen, ulichan, and uthlecan. Oolichan is often pronounced "hooligan", and it is also widely
known as "candlefish", from its reputed ability to be stood on
end and burned, with a wick like a candle, because it's so oily.
On the lower Fraser, the Sto:lo people called them swavie, and
they nicknamed them chucka, which means "old woman". In the
early days of the maritime fur trade, ships' captains called them
"shrow", and the grease from the fish was called "shrow tow",
words that appear to have been derived from the Haida words
for oolichan and oolichan grease, a product the Haida obtained
by trade every spring, in massive quantities, from their mainland
neighbours, the Nisga'a. Central Coast Natives sometimes called
oolichan the "salvation fish", for the fact that the oolichan's
arrival after a long, cold winter provided the year's first great
flourish of fresh marine flesh, certain salvation if the winter had
been particularly rough. Their arrival was a sure sign that winter
was truly gone, that it was not the end of the world, and that the
cycle of the seasons could begin again. Salvation fish became
"saviour fish" in some Central Coast communities, which was
pleasing to the first Methodist missionaries until it became
apparent that the oolichan's ascent from the sea, triggered partly
by river temperature and partly by the tide (which is itself determined by the phases of the moon), tended to coincide with
Easter. Easter Sunday always falls on the first Sunday after the

paschal full moon, which is the first full moon after March 21, so the arrival of the oolichan often meant deserted church pews on the holiest day of the liturgical calendar, because everybody was away "making grease".

Howard White, who first came upon the substance in Bella Bella in 1976 at $48 a gallon, wrote that

> ... it smelled like the cracks
> between the deck planks of an old fish barge
> if you can imagine spreading that
> on your bread – quite enough to hurl
> the European palate toward the nearest
> toilet bowl ...

As a consequence, there wasn't much of a non-aboriginal market for the fish, and there had been little scientific interest in it, and not much was known about its life history or the role the oolichan played in marine ecosystems. So when things began to go haywire among the various populations of Osmeridae, specifically among oolichan populations, all DFO's biologists could turn to was a body of scientific literature you could fit in a desk drawer. The generally held wisdom about oolichans was that they probably returned to their natal streams to spawn, but not necessarily; that they tended to spawn at two or three years of age, mainly (but not always) in rivers that were formed from glacier-fed creeks along the mainland coast; and that they seemed to die after spawning, the way salmon do, but not necessarily all of them. Morley Farwell, the DFO management biologist who was in charge of the Fraser River oolichan fishery in the 1980s, used to joke that his decisions about oolichan openings consisted of looking out the window of his New Westminster offices in late March to see if there were lots of seagulls around.

Except for the Nass River – which gets its name from the Tlin-git word for "food depot", after the great oolichan harvests near the river's mouth – oolichan runs coast-wide appear to have begun a fairly rapid descent about 1985, after a period of local-ized declines. These things went largely unnoticed by DFO officials, and those who had their suspicions were unwilling to attempt a guess at the extent of the declines, partly because fisheries' records were either nonexistent or based almost solely on hunches, guesses, and rumour. On the Fraser River, commer-cial catches dropped from 329,000 pounds annually in the early 1960s to less than 100,000 pounds through the 1970s and about 50,000 pounds in the 1980s. DFO scientists conceded that they didn't know how much these declines reflected shifts in market demand or reduced catch effort, but the fishermen on the river were insisting that there were just way fewer oolichans around and the seals and the sea lions had begun to fight them for what was left. Upriver, Sto:lo fishermen were complaining that oolichans that used to run beyond Agassiz were no longer mak-ing it even two-thirds that far, to Mission (in the 1940s, fisheries scientists were sure that the short stretch of river from Mission up to Deroche was the main spawning area for the fish). Chawathil elder Bill Pat Charlie remembered joining in the annual fishery, when Sto:lo families scooped huge buckets of fresh oolichan from behind a sandbar below the old Saint Mary's residential school, "but then they just stopped coming" some time around the mid-1980s. "Used to be that only thunder and lightning would scare them away, but then they didn't come so far. They just started dying away."

Even as far downriver as the Katzie village in Pitt Meadows, something was changing, and the changes were particularly omi-nous because it was at that very spot in the river, just off what is now the foot of Bonson Road where the reserve is, that oolichans first appeared in this world, in the first few years after human beings were placed on the earth. According to Katzie traditions, the oolichan came from the dowry box brought to earth by the sky-born wife of Swaneset, who is sort of a Katzie version of Moses. In Old Pierre's account of the first oolichan, which he related to the anthropologist Diamond Jenness in 1936:

> The people gathered at the river to witness the opening of the box, which was divided by a partition into two parts. Swaneset's wife opened one part first. Instantly a cloud of feathers flew up into the air and changed to sea-gulls, which soared up and down the Fraser River just as they do today. The woman then turned homeward, saying to her husband, "I will open the other half tomorrow."
>
> At daybreak she opened the other half of the box and emptied its contents into the river. Forthwith immense shoals of eulachon crowded the water from bank to bank. She waited until the sun rose, then ordered the people to rake the fish into their canoes.
>
> "For one month only each year will these fish appear," she said. "Gather them diligently ... "

As late as the 1960s, as many as eighty Katzie people were busy at oolichan time, fishing from boats and working in dock crews, picking nets and packing fish in boxes for the local markets. Even as recently as 1990, as many as a dozen Katzie people were busy every spring for the two or three weeks that the oolichans ran in the river, and at twelve oolichans to a pound and $1.50 a pound, it meant reasonable wages in the long months before the sockeye runs. Back then, the oolichans were still running thick and heavy, and the sky was filled with seagulls. Then everything started to change.

On a spring day in 1995 at Katzie, Jimmy Adams, Mark Petrunia's upriver test-fishery colleague, stood on the reserve's rickety dock and pointed to the sea lions gathering in the river just behind a log boom. "See? When I go out to do one of these test sets, they're waiting for me, the bastards. When I go downriver, they follow me. They follow me all the way down. They go right through the net. They bite right through the net. They won't leave me alone."

Beginning in about 1990, the annual Fraser River catch had fallen to 20,000 pounds, less than a fifteenth of the 1960s catch. Then in 1994, everybody's nets were coming up empty. The Musqueam fishermen staged a protest and called for a fishing closure. Alarm bells started to go off at DFO, and for the first time in history, the Fraser River oolichan fishery was shut down in-season.

Meanwhile, on the Columbia River, an even more dramatic event was occurring. In 1994, hardly any oolichan were caught at all in the Columbia or its tributaries. The total catch was ninety-five percent below average, almost a total loss. But in the nearby Wynoochee, the river was thick with oolichan, and nobody had ever seen them spawn there before.

On the Central Coast that year, the unimaginable happened. In late March, Nimpkish fisherman Stephen Beans and his family headed out in their seine boat, the *Ocean Predator*, for the season's fishing and grease-making up Knight Inlet. But day after day went by and there was no sign of oolichan anywhere. The days turned into weeks. Families from Alert Bay and other Kwagewlth communities waited at their Knight Inlet fishing camps, but no oolichan came home. For Beans, it was the first time anything like it had happened in the thirty-five years he had been fishing. Runs had been dropping drastically in the King-come River for four or five years, but none of the old people could remember anything quite like this. The Klinaklini River, which takes its name from the Kwakwala term meaning "lots of grease", was barren.

The oolichan were gone.

"It was a total failure," Beans said. "Up here, we depend quite a lot on the oolichans. When they come, we stop everything we're doing for it. Up Knight Inlet, you'll have maybe half a dozen to a dozen families, maybe fifty to eighty people. All over this part of the coast, people depend on us to supply them. So it was really hard, because it's really a necessity, and you can't put a dollar figure on it. We had a hard time coming home and telling people 'No.' "

There was a lot of harsh talk about Interfor's logging practices in the Klinaklini Valley. Farther north, on the Kitimat River, the Eurocan pulp mill was an obvious contributor to the declines up there. Pacific white-sided dolphins had been moving into Knight Inlet by the hundreds, and they'd never been seen there before. There was a new pollock trawl fishery in Johnstone Strait, and nobody at DFO knew what its incidental catch of oolichan might have been, but DFO's own surveys showed that in the shrimp-trawl fisheries, oolichans and other nontarget fish were showing up in nets. In 1991, a DFO survey showed that seventy percent of the shrimp-trawl catch was nontarget species, primarily oolichans and dogfish that ended up thrown back and wasted, and a 1992 survey concluded that only ten percent of the shrimpers' overall catch was actually shrimp.

At the Pacific Biological Station, research scientist Doug Hay was trying to add it all up, and by the spring of 1995, none of it was making all that much sense. No single culprit could be to blame, Hay reckoned, and it didn't make sense that a whole range of culprits could conspire to gang up on oolichans throughout the coast, all at different times. What seemed to make more sense was that something was happening in the ocean, something as subtle as changes in ocean temperature during the summer months while the coast's oolichan populations – many, if not most, of them, anyway – were in the midst of their migrations, somewhere near the edge of the continental shelf, say, off the west coast of Vancouver Island. But Hay said: "If you're asking me what's going on, the answer is 'I don't know,' and I don't think anybody does."

The smart thing to do seemed to be to establish some greater certainty about the oolichans' life histories: Where, exactly, do they spawn in the Fraser River, for instance? How long does it take the egg to grow to larval stage, get washed out to saltwater, and start migrating seaward? Where do they go? How long do they live? How does something so small, something that seems to get washed out to sea so quickly, remember its natal river? Do they always come back to their natal rivers? How many of them die after spawning? Can they spawn twice?

To begin to find answers to these questions, the fisheries research vessel *W. E. Ricker* was sent out off Vancouver Island's west coast to look for migrating oolichan. For several weeks in 1995, the *Reviser* was dragging a trawl net – with tiny, tiny mesh – at seventeen different sites up and down the Fraser River, fishing for oolichan larvae. Mark Petrunia, Jimmy Adams, and Harold Wolf were out with the seals and sea lions, conducting test sets at their spots in the Fraser. And up at the head of Knight Inlet, biologist Mike Berry, whose childhood was spent hanging around the edges of Haisla oolichan camps and snorkelling down the Kitimat River for lost lures to sell back to steelhead fishermen, was busy trying to come to grips with the tragedy on the Klinaklini.

Berry was working for the Tanakteuk band, which holds ancestral villages at the head of Knight Inlet, so when he began his research in 1995, he knew it was serious business. Oolichans mean everything to the Tanakteuk. So Berry threw himself into the work, assembled everything he'd ever done on oolichans, reviewed aerial photographs of the Klinaklini River to assess potential logging damage to the spawning grounds, set up a system to analyze the flow regime in the river and check it against rainfall records, filled jar after jar with various specimens, assembled counts of the white-sided dolphins that started showing up in the inlet about four years ago, set up transects on the Klinaklini and nearby rivers, and settled down into camp with all the Kwagewlths who had arrived in hope that the oolichan would come back.

The days went by and no oolichan showed. Everybody's mood was grim. People from Nimpkish and Campbell River and Alert Bay sat around in their camps with nothing much to do, while seventy-two-year-old Charlie Matilpy sat at the mouth of the Klinaklini and sang mournful songs in Kwakwala, asking the oolichan to come home.

On Good Friday, there were 214 Pacific white-sided dolphins in Knight Inlet. On Saturday, the dolphins turned down the inlet and disappeared somewhere around the Broughton Archipelago.

On Easter Sunday morning, the oolichan came home.

"It was unbelievable," Berry remembered. "It was like gangbusters. The sun was shining; the people were so incredibly happy. Everybody was on cloud nine. It was beautiful."

Over at the Kingcome River, where hardly any fish had been seen in four years, it was the same thing. On the nearby Franklin River, never a big oolichan river, "it was absolutely chockablock plugged," Berry said. A count of eight thousand square metres of river bottom turned up a hundred fish per square metre, which adds up to 800,000 fish. On the Columbia River, catches were way up over 1994. The Nass fishery was tremendous, as always. On the other northern rivers, abundance seemed to be holding, at least, and on the Fraser River, there were big changes: logbooks were made mandatory for the commercial fishermen; they had to report the catches on a weekly basis; and the commercial openings for Mark Petrunia and his fellow oolichan gillnetters were cut back from six days a week to three, a plan that Petrunia would fairly shout about if you asked him his opinion. He said it was a completely bonehead deal.

But if you asked him how he did in 1995, Petrunia would tell you he figured he'd caught about 5,000 pounds in half the time it took to catch 3,500 pounds the year before. DFO management biologist Marilyn Joyce reported that everybody's catches were up in the Fraser, and Cheam band fisherman Isaac Alex saw oolichans jumping in the river, way beyond Mission, just past the Rosedale Bridge, near Agassiz.

"And if it wasn't for the goddamned seals and the goddamned sea lions, I'd have caught a lot more," Petrunia said.

Out with Petrunia on his gillnet boat, the day's test fishery took longer than usual. The run was nearly over, and it took two sets to get the hundred-fish minimum the fisheries scientists wanted. There were fewer seals around, and hardly any sea lions, so less than one quarter of the fish Petrunia caught came up half-eaten. When we got back to his dock in Annacis Channel, just as he was tying off the *Escorial II*, Petrunia said: "I make grease too, you know. First time, this year. Want to try some?"

I'd had grease before. The first time, it was just a little bit on the side of a plate of smoked seal meat, barbecued salmon, and salad at a Nisga'a get-together in Prince Rupert, eight years before. There had been a huge bowl of it on the serving table, and I took just the tiniest bit to see what it was like. It was only a taste. It was indescribable, true enough, but after a moment or two it didn't seem anything near as horrible as I'd been led to expect, so I went back for more. But by then it was all gone, and the sides of the bowl had been scraped clean, and all around the hall, the people were eating silently and smiling. It was like being in church.

In Howard White's poem "Oolachon Grease", the degree to which white people recoil from the substance is supposed to be a measure of something important, and it is

... how far
Indian is from White how far
learning is from knowing how
far we are from this ragged place
we've taken from them ...

Barry Manuck, an old friend, a gillnetter, skipper of the Panther, dropped by Petrunia's place for a chat. The three of us sat in the kitchen, and in the living room, Mark's wife, Mary, and their kids, Matthew, Willy, Chrissy, and Samantha, were watching something on television. So there we were, three white guys sitting at the kitchen table, and between us sat a huge glass jar full of an extremely primitive form of oolichan grease Petrunia had cooked up in a steel pot on a Coleman stove beside his shed on the dyke.

After waiting to see who'd go first, Petrunia opened the jar and helped himself to a spoonful.

"It's good. See?"

Then it was my turn. It was a bit startling at first, but certainly tame compared to the real stuff as I remembered it. It was actually pretty good. A lot like sockeye belly oil. Tasty.

Then it was Manuck's turn.

"You know, it's not bad," Manuck said.

and however far you are from loving that
is how far you are
                    from arriving

Or so the poem goes.

"I think I could have this with, I don't know, rice, maybe," Manuck said.

Petrunia said he thought that was a good idea. He took another heaping spoonful and passed the jar around again.

"See?" he said. "Excellent."